www.united-pc.eu

My Adventure with Dementia

An aide to dementia, self-help and a tale of life and adventure

By Vicki Binley

Contents Page

Dedication

This book is written in dedication to my father who had the long drawn out loss of memory with Alzheimer's, and for all others who are suffering this awful disease. From this once strong, exceptionally proud, vibrant, filled a room with his presence, sociable, kind, argumentative father, grandfather and husband to a shadow of his former self (semi shell), I struggled with all of it, the disease and what to do when. I felt it was time to write this guide and help others who are having an adventure with dementia, remember the funny times, write down the memories both past and present and try to ignore the sad.

The purpose of writing this book is as an aid to coping, a self-help book, plus a homage to my father. I have found it an ordeal dealing with the disease and my dad's deterioration plus working with the systems and laws, so this is my attempt to help all those who need to make those life changing decisions.

But above all, it is to say dementia is not all doom and gloom, there are moments when one achieves enriching experiences which would not have happened without the disease.

ALZHEIMER'S POEM (love this poem and it helped me to remember why, until the end)

Do not ask me to remember

Do not try to make me understand

Let me rest and know you're with me

Kiss my cheek and hold my hand.

I'm confused beyond your concept

I am sad and sick and lost.

All I know is that I need you

To be with me at all cost.

Do not lose your patience with me

Do not scold or curse my cry

I can't help the way I'm acting

Can't be different though I try

Just remember that I need you,

That the best of me is gone,

Please don't fail to stand beside me,

Love me till my life is done.

(anonymous)

INTRO

My adventure began in 2005, but first I want to tell you about my father.

My father was born in 1930, in Pontypool, Wales but lived his formative years in Bristol. He had two sisters, one older and one younger, to an older father (a builder) who was of the Victorian era of show no feelings, never cry, stiff upper lip (spare the rod, spoil the child), (children should be seen but never heard). As the only boy he appeared to bear the brunt of punishments and was often given the belt for misdemeanours we would laugh at nowadays, but beside this he had a lot of freedom which many did not have. He did not show affection as many of that generation did not, they do not cry or show weakness, but we always knew he cared. He was an adventurer in his own way and was scared of nothing as far as I could work out except for being ill. All my life he weightlifted, sailed, ran, rode motor bikes, skied, cycled, but never played any team sports except water polo. He loved travelling, and when he retired he and my mother sailed for 15 years around the Mediterranean and across the Atlantic to the Caribbean, USA, Newfoundland. So amazing!

Life should be an adventure!

CHAPTER 1- What is it?

Dementia

There are 850,000 people with dementia in the UK, with numbers set to rise to over one million by 2025. This will soar to two million by 2051. 225,000 will develop dementia this year, that's one every three minutes. (Alzheimer's UK)

a. Definition

Dementia is a loss of mental ability severe enough to interfere with normal activities of daily living, lasting more than six months, not present since birth, and not associated with a loss or alteration of consciousness. (Medical dictionary)

A chronic or persistent disorder of the mental processes caused by brain disease or injury and marked by memory disorders, personality changes, and impaired reasoning. (Oxford dictionary)

b. Description

Dementia is a group of symptoms caused by gradual death of brain cells. Society uses this word to cover all the conditions from mild to seriously impaired. It is the loss of cognitive abilities that occurs with dementia leading to diminishing loss in memory, reasoning, planning, and behaviour. While the overwhelming number of people with dementia are elderly, dementia is not an inevitable part of ageing; instead, dementia is caused by specific brain diseases. Alzheimer's disease (AD) is the most common cause, followed by vascular or multi infarct dementia, there are numerous types of dementia all with slightly differing symptoms and speed of progression.

I am not going into detail here as there are numerous websites and books which give you descriptions, scientific analysis and any research, which is now fortunately starting to increase as dementia appears to be on the increase, and not just with retired folk as once thought. Ages are getting much younger, now even in the thirties and forties. It is also a disease that affects all walks of life, many famous people have suffered with it, Margaret Thatcher (Politician), Ronald Reagan (actor/US President), Charlton Heston (actor), Perry Como (singer) Glen Cambell (musician), Malcolm Young (AC/DC) Terry Pratchett (author). Dementia crosses all spectrums of society, rich or poor.

Vascular dementia appears to be the main type that is identified and can start suddenly or come on slowly over time (many people with vascular dementia also have Alzheimer's). This is the one my dad had.

These problems can make daily activities increasingly difficult and someone with the condition may eventually be unable to look after themselves.

c. Causes

Dementia is usually caused by degeneration in the cerebral cortex, the part of the brain responsible for thoughts, memories, actions, and personality. Death of brain cells in this region leads to the cognitive impairment that characterizes dementia.

The most common form of dementia is AD (Alzheimer's disease) accounting for one-half to three-fourths of all cases. The brain of a person with AD becomes clogged with two abnormal structures called neurofibrillary tangles and senile plaques. Seen on an x-ray the areas affected are black as the nerves and cells die off. Why these structures develop is unknown. Scientists now blame smoking, alcohol, bad diet and lack of exercise, but personally I don't think it is any of these as my father was fit, never smoked, drank minimally and exercised every day until he forgot how. I believe in years to come it will be the food we eat and chemicals. I also think stress is a huge influencing factor.

Other conditions that may cause dementia include:

- AIDS

- Parkinson's disease

- Lewy body disease

- Pick's disease

- Huntington's disease

- Creutzfeldt-Jakob disease

- Brain tumour

- Hydrocephalus

- Head trauma

- Multiple sclerosis

- Prolonged abuse of alcohol or other drugs

- Vitamin deficiency: thiamin, niacin, or B_{12}

- Hypothyroidism

- Hypercalcemia

d. <u>Symptoms</u>

Dementia is marked by a gradual deterioration of thought and other mental activities. They judge it on seven stages (see figures 1 & 2 for a rough timeline). Loss eventually affects virtually every aspect of mental life, day-to-day memory – for example, difficulty recalling events that happened recently, following the plot in a film or reading a book, and as the disease progresses the person cannot recall the previous reading so tend to give up reading books and watching films.

It may begin with misplacing valuables such as a wallet or car keys, then progress to forgetting appointments, where the car is parked or even the route home. This should be on a regular basis not just occasionally as we all do this at times with stress and modern living.

Language skills – for example, difficulties following a conversation or finding the right word for something, being unable to understand instructions or follow the logic of moderately complex sentences. Later, the individual may not understand his or her own sentences and have difficulty forming thoughts into words. This can also happen with those without dementia if they are nervous, for example. So don't panic, if you are like me and keep misplacing items.

I have included the two scales below as they may help the way forward. The timeline is only a guide and not completely accurate. Many of dad's symptoms were earlier than in the chart. Each person is different, I believe.

The most commonly used scale for judging the level of Alzheimer's is often referred to simply as GDS, or by its more formal name, the Reisberg Scale or even by the lengthy name Global Deterioration Scale for Assessment.

The GDS scale divides the disease process into seven stages based on the amount of cognitive decline in the inflicted person. This test is most relevant for people who have Alzheimer's disease since some other types of dementia (i.e. Frontotemporal dementia) do not always include memory loss

Figure 1. Reisberg's stages of Alzheimer's

Reisberg's Stages (also called Global Deterioration S			
1 No Cognitive Decline	**2 Very Mild Cognitive Decline**	**3 Mild Cognitive Decline**	**4 Mo Cogniti**
• No complaints of memory problems • No evidence of cognitive deficits	• Reports of memory problems, like misplacing objects or forgetting names • No evidence of issues with work or social situations	• Impaired concentration • Difficulty with work tasks • Some denial and anxiety about the deficits	• Trouble reme personal histo • Trouble trave or handling fin • Reduced exp of emotions • Withdrawal fr that are challe
5 Moderately Severe Cognitive Decline	**6 Severe Cognitive Decline**		**7 Very Cognitiv**
• Some assistance needed • Evidence of short-term memory loss • Lack of orientation to time, place, or date • May need assistance with choosing what to wear	• Lack of awareness of recent activities or surroundings • Activities of daily living may require assistance • Evidence of incontinence and or bowel issues • Sleep disturbances • Personality and behavior changes occur, including hallucinations, anxiety, agitation, and obsessive behavior		• Significant pe and behavior c • Loss of speec to hold a conve • Difficulty mov and swallowing • Loss of bladde control • Unable to do o without assista

AlzheimersDisease.ne

Figure 2

Global Deterioration Scale (CGS) / Reisberg Scale			
Diagnosis	Stage	Signs and Symptoms	Expected Duration of Stage
No Dementia	Stage 1: No Cognitive Decline	In this stage, the person functions normally, has no memory loss, and is mentally healthy. People with NO dementia would be considered to be in Stage 1.	N/A
No Dementia	Stage 2: Very Mild Cognitive Decline	This stage is used to describe normal forgetfulness associated with aging.	Unknown

		For example, forgetting names and where familiar objects were left. Symptoms of dementia are not evident to the individual's loved ones or their physician.	
No Dementia	Stage 3: Mild Cognitive Decline	This stage includes increased forgetfulness, slight difficulty concentrating, and decreased work performance. People may get lost more frequently or have difficulty finding the right words. At this stage, a person's loved ones will begin to	Average duration of this stage is between 2 years and 7 years.

		notice a cognitive decline.	
Early-stage	Stage 4: Moderate Cognitive Decline	This stage includes difficulty concentrating, decreased memory of recent events, and difficulties managing finances or traveling alone to new locations. People have trouble completing complex tasks efficiently or accurately and may be in denial about their symptoms. They may also start withdrawing from family or friends because socialization becomes	Average duration of this stage is 2 years.

		difficult. At this stage, a physician can detect clear cognitive problems during a patient interview and exam.	
Mid-Stage	Stage 5: Moderately Severe Cognitive Decline	People in this stage have major memory deficiencies and need some assistance to complete their daily living activities (dressing, bathing, preparing meals, etc.). Memory loss is more prominent and may include major relevant aspects of current lives. For example,	Average duration of this stage is 1.5 years.

		people may not remember their address or phone number and may not know the time or day or where they are.	
Mid-Stage	Stage 6: Severe Cognitive Decline (Middle Dementia)	People in Stage 6 require extensive assistance to carry out their Activities of Daily Living (ADLs). They start to forget names of close family members and have little memory of recent events. Many people can remember only some details of earlier life. Individuals also have difficulty	Average duration of this stage is 2.5 years

		counting down from 10 and finishing tasks. Incontinence (loss of bladder or bowel control) is a problem in this stage. Ability to speak declines. Personality / emotional changes, such as delusions (believing something to be true that is not), compulsions (repeating a simple behavior, such as cleaning), or anxiety and agitation may occur.	
Late-Stage	Stage 7: Very Severe	People in this stage have essentially no	Average duration of this

	Cognitive Decline (Late Dementia)	ability to speak or communicate. They require assistance with most activities (e.g., using the toilet, eating). They often lose psychomotor skills. For example, the ability to walk.	stage is 1.5 to 2.5 years.

(https://www.dementiacarecentral.com)

The person may not be able to identify the time of day, even from obvious visual clues, losing track of the day or date, or becoming confused about where they are, even if familiar.

Poor judgement. The person with dementia may not recognize the consequences of his or her actions or be able to evaluate the appropriateness of behaviour or level of risk. Common examples include opening the door to strangers and not seeing any risk, answering the phone to marketing calls and booking appointments, or giving away personal details and not appreciating the consequences.

Personal hygiene may be ignored. They seem to dislike water and touch as time progresses.

Problems with concentrating, planning or organising and understanding – for example, difficulties making decisions, solving problems or carrying out a sequence of tasks. For example, when cooking a meal, they become distracted and wander away, there was many a burnt pan in our house and the risk of fire or the gas flame going out and the gas remaining on.

Some, but not all, get increased restlessness. This may cause the person with dementia to begin an activity and quickly lose interest and/or to wander frequently. Wandering may create significant safety problems when combined with disorientation and can lead to going for a walk and not being able to find their way home. Finally, difficulty walking and keeping their balance.

Sleep disturbances may occur, including insomnia and sleep interruptions, falling out of bed, or wandering in the night and not finding the bedroom, this happened to my dad on staying in hotels and been locked in the corridor as would go wandering for the toilet (even though en-suite) and be locked out.

Repetitive questions asked again and again.

Judging distances becomes a problem (such as on stairs) and seeing objects in three dimensions, walking into things or seeing things differently to how we see them, i.e their hands come up and move in front of them as if something is there. They become disorientated and confused.

Mood and behavioral changes and psychosis. Behaviour may become rude, overly friendly, or aggressive. The person with dementia may lose interest in once-pleasurable activities and become more passive, depressed, or anxious. Delusions, suspicion, paranoia, and hallucinations may occur. In the case of my father he would not move as the disease progressed. I was unsure if he was frightened or just forgot to get up. Each case is so different.

Sundowning is a word that many apply for the changes in behaviour that occur in the evening, around dusk. Some people who have been diagnosed with dementia experience a growing sense of agitation or anxiety at this time. Sundowning symptoms might include a compelling sense that they are in the wrong place. I was lucky my dad did not appear to get this but many do.

e. Memory tests

On the internet are loads of sites offering to do a memory test, I DO NOT recommend this course of action as there is no true test online to determine if you have dementia. Memory loss could be for many other health reasons. Best course of action is to go to your GP who will do tests and follow up.

Memory cafes are appearing in most towns and villages now so if you are worried, go to one of these and seek advice as many different agencies attend these to give out help and information.

f. Communication

Try not to contradict or correct them if they say something wrong. If they're alert enough, they'll realize they made a mistake and feel bad about it. Even if they don't understand their error, correcting them may embarrass or be otherwise unpleasant for them.

Try not to argue with the person. It's never a good idea to argue with a person who has dementia. First, you can't win. And second, it will probably upset them or even make them angry. Try to change the subject preferably to something pleasant that will immediately catch their attention. That way, hopefully, they'll likely forget all about the disagreement.

Try not to ask "Do you remember…". When talking with a person who has Alzheimer's, it's so tempting to ask them if they remember some person or event. "What did you have for lunch?" "What did you do this morning?" "Do you remember that TV programme we watched when I visited last week?" "This is Aunt Joan, do you remember her?" Of course, they don't remember. Otherwise, they wouldn't have a diagnosis of dementia. It is frustrating for them if they don't remember. Reminisce instead, give them huge clues. I always went in and said "Hi Dad", so he knew it was his daughter, although even then sometimes he did not know me, it depended on what era he was in I think.

It's not uncommon for people with dementia to believe their deceased spouse, parent or other loved one is still alive. They may be confused or feel hurt that the person doesn't come to visit. If you inform them that the person is dead, they might not believe it and become angry with you. If they do believe you, they may grieve all over again. What's more, they're likely to soon forget what you said and go back to believing their loved one is still alive, so say they are out at the moment, shopping or visiting someone. An exception to this, is if they ask you if the person is gone. Then it's wise to give them an honest answer, even if they will soon forget it, and then go on to some other topic.

There's no reason to bring up topics you know may upset your loved one. If you don't see eye-to eye on politics, for example, don't even bring it up. It may just start an argument, which goes against the second guideline above. You won't win and it's just likely to cause them anger and/or frustration.

Try not to say "You have just asked me that" after they have said something numerous times. Just patiently repeat. I know it is frustrating but if it annoys you too much try to redirect their attention elsewhere.

Never say "You cannot do that", guide them to what they can do.

Never demand – always ask.

Basically, I believe you should go into their world, their reality. It might seem odd, but go along with it. Many times, I went to see dad, and he said "How did you find me in France (or Australia)?" I made something up like "Just visiting", or "Just flew in". Normally they are somewhere they are familiar with. In a meeting, at a gathering, airport, in a supermarket; they try to fit something to understand the scenario. Their reality is real to them and they are living it.

g. Vulnerability

As with any person with a mental illness, they become very vulnerable and prey to those not so good in the world.

Usually it is for their money.

Many vulnerable adults suddenly acquire 'friends'. They offer friendship or to do you a favour, they offer to buy something off you as a favour to get it off your hands, they request bank details to go to the cash point so they can run errands for you.

Often the best course of action is to limit money available to them, if you have bank access. Then if this happens hopefully the loss is limited.

Phone call hazards - cold callers on the phone, who made appointments with dad who then forgot. In our case luckily the carer heard him on the phone so I was able to call back and cancel the appointment for double glazing and another for an attic inspection. A way round this is to try to stop cold callers, but even with all the technology available this is not guaranteed. BT appears to be the best with 'call guardian'.

My father handed over bank account numbers so lost money from the bank. Luckily in our case the bank refunded the money but others are not so lucky.

h. My dad's history

My mother had concerns about my father's memory prior to her death, 15 years ago, and said he was changing, his memory was not at it was, but could not specify. His navigation skills were going and putting them at risk whilst sailing. As with most people at the onset of dementia they refuse to believe anything is untoward or that they need to see a doctor. They carry on with life and do so with no outward signs of the impending struggle to come.

I'm not sure when the dementia took hold properly, but little give away clues in change of personality crept in in subtle little ways, but to others he would appear fine. (I often noted more in hindsight). I believe those who know them best see the signs first. I often wonder if it was brought on by grief of my mother dying. He would not show emotion and did not visibly grieve, just got on with life as if nothing was different.

He met and got involved with a lady within six months of my mother's death (whilst attending a bereavement group). This seemed out of character, but he took her sailing, carrying out exactly the same routines and all the activities he had done with my mother. To me one of the first signs of his diminishing health was calling his grandson his nephew. Many parts of his family history he was telling his now new wife were inaccurate, but it was difficult to argue, or disagree without appearing churlish and bad mannered.

He had his driving licence removed from him, I never knew the full facts of how or why, but it was a big downturn in attitude. He then started getting bouts of bad temper, (frustration, I think) then, not getting out of bed at all, appearing depressed rather than with dementia. He developed an aversion to washing when he always without fail every day previously would have had an army wash, in cold water of course! He would forget to go to bed, staying up all night and falling asleep in the chair and not being rested at all. He would sit around with no clothes on and no encouragement would get him to put them on. All these symptoms at first were put down to depression and the doctors seemed disinclined to offer the diagnosis of dementia. He did not get a diagnosis for years after the symptoms began. He went for specialist tests but seemed to pass these. Dementia patients can still be shrewd.

He had always loved going for a walk, We were out one day on one of our regular walks and he looked at me and said laughingly, "Good job you're with me as I would not be able to find my way back."

His normal habits began to slide, his exercise stopped (previously he had always got out of bed and done sit ups, push-ups and stretches), house maintenance stopped. His love of reading went. He finally let on in one of his honest moments that it was a waste of time as he could not remember the previous chapters. The same with TV and regular series with plots and dramas, so he stopped watching. Other symptoms were grinding of teeth. Loss of dental hygiene. Wringing of hands. Finally, not moving, everything needed coaxing. He would just sit, forget to eat or drink unless offered and even then, would forget.

He did not like shaving anymore and was growing a beard, so to try and make life normal we took him to an understanding barber explaining the situation first – he was lovely – and managed to give him a great haircut and trim his beard.

He got bladder incontinence and would lie in bed wet and would not notice, he would wet himself wherever. He would not wear pads, so I tried to buy cotton pants with extra thickness so that they felt normal, but this was a dismal failure - he still would not wear them. You would find incontinence pads ripped up all over the floor. I used to put puppy pads on all the chairs disguised with a throw to stop the furniture being ruined. Some days it was as if there was nothing wrong, he would revert to his old self, but others days you would be talking and then you could visibly see the mist roll in and the memory going resulting in loss of confidence and fear of going out. He still liked being taken for car drives anywhere and he always appeared more alert and interactive after these.

One of the scenarios my son found the funniest was if he was visiting and dad and his wife had a falling out (she was in denial that he was ill, she thought it was deliberate) but he would then wander into another room and forget all the previous disagreement and she would wander in still angry and dad would ask "What is the matter, why are you upset?" It is a very difficult illness to live with without a very good sense of humour and lots of love.

The other funny thing was mirrors. Every time he looked in one, he could not believe it was him, he would get upset, "is that me"? In the care home mirrors were very limited, but there was one in the lift. So on one occasion he looked with horror for the whole lift journey not believing it was him. I think this is because people with dementia see themselves in a different era to reality.

Chapter 2

Caring at Home

People affected by dementia often face loneliness and social exclusion, as they cut themselves off from the outside world from embarrassment, shame, confusion, and not wishing to be a nuisance.

It is nicer if you can keep the person at home for as long as possible in their own surroundings with all the things they know and love around them, but this depends on if there is a family/carer at home to support them.

They need to keep up with hobbies and interests, go for a walk, do gardening, listen to music. Research has proved this helps them out of themselves, even a pint down the local is helpful as they are meeting all the regulars they usually see, plus chatting and being social, all keeping the person happy. And helping the brain fire a few neurons!

As dad would not get out of his chair, and then struggled and needed a helping pull to get him to standing we rushed out and purchased a tilt and rise chair. It was brilliant for a while; he could not use the controls but it helped us and the carers to encourage him to move, and saved our backs.

They need good nutrition and plenty of fluids to prevent dehydration or a kidney infection quickly follows and may need respite care, this happened to my dad, he was not drinking enough fluids being on his own most of the day and no way to keep his fluid Intake up. I later learnt, jellies, custard, rice pudding etc, have a lot of fluid so even if not drinking they are getting fluid in them. If they do not have enough fluids, they are prone to urine infections which can make them hallucinate.

Washing them can be difficult as they appear to go anti water. One day we managed to get dad in the shower and happily had all his clean clothes ready for him to put on. When he came out fully dressed in all his smelly clothes, oops, lesson learned, the minute they are undressed nip in and remove them for the wash.

Communicate clearly, i.e. don't ask multiple questions in one statement. This was my big failing, just ask simple questions which require a yes or no, as per previous chapter. I tended to drown him in questions and get a shrug as a response. Keep it simple.

All information which you read states write things down, write lists, leave post-its but in my experience, they forget to read them. A list of useful aids to help with memory are in chapter 8.

For an emergency, personal alarms might be a good idea. I thought about one of these for my dad, but they must agree to keep it on their person, but Dad would not wear it round his neck or on his wrist. There are various levels of cover as in all insurance, it is all dependent on how much you can afford or wish to pay, but some devices can send an alarm to the provider after a fall. There are many devices on the market. Age Concern do one at approx. £120 plus £60 a quarter, Lifeline have one for a monthly charge. There are Telecare systems which are designed to send a warning to a call centre or carer if there is a problem in the home – in risk areas such as falls, inactivity, fire, floods or gas leaks. By remotely monitoring an older person's activity and other factors in their home, the technology helps to keep them safe and independent. It also provides reassurance to family and friends who may not be able to call in as often as they would like.

There is a growth in remote healthcare called Telehealth which provides remote access to some health care services for people with long-term health conditions. Using a combination of equipment and technology, Telehealth makes it possible for medical professionals to monitor your health, manage your treatment or diagnose conditions without you needing to visit a surgery or arrange a home visit. The technology is sometimes also called Telemedicine.

Agencies

Caring at home for someone with a long-term illness/condition can last many years so if you can plan ahead a little it might help.

There are many agencies out there to help support people in their home and the first start would be the social services in your area. Your GP can always advise on the first step, it is after this that life can get difficult.

Home help is usually available from the local Council and it is also possible to pay privately for carers, if you have the funds and would like specific help. Home help can help with washing and dressing, help with shopping, help with housework and help with medication, if for instance another long-term condition is involved i.e Diabetes, to ensure correct dosage and regular medication.

What to expect if you or a member of your family asks for assistance from your local authority social services department or if another professional asks a social worker to visit because they have concerns about the welfare of a member of your family? To find the number for your local social services you will need to contact your local authority.

Local authority adult or children's social services support family members who have additional needs beyond what health, education or community services can help with. They also have a duty to safeguard children and vulnerable adults who may be at risk of harm, whether from family members or others. Levels of support can vary within each local authority and although the law defines what their duties are, they also have their own 'thresholds' as to when they will provide a service.

Social services have a statutory obligation to safeguard and promote the welfare of vulnerable children and adults and can provide a wide range of services, usually within the own home environment and co-ordinated by a social worker. A social worker is usually assigned to your case. Families often feel anxious at the prospect of social services involvement because of experiences they may have heard from others, or just because they are frightened that social will intervene and take over. I found them very helpful and compassionate with useful advice.

There are many different departments in social services to support varying needs. There is an adult social services department, which provides services to the elderly and working age adults who have learning difficulties, physical or mental health problems, or addictions. It was adult social services I called first and would advise if you have a problem and they are elderly. If a child is looking after a parent with a disability, they might be referred to as a 'young carer' and there may be special provisions in place to help if this is the situation. Often, social care services for adults who have a mental illness, or an addiction, are provided by a mental health trust.

It is common for these different departments to work together if a family or individual need this. The aim is to coordinate their services in the interests of the family as a whole.

Referrals to social services can happen in a number of ways. You can request help yourself by calling your local social services. Referrals can be made by other professionals who are working with your family such as GPs, health visitors, teachers.

Depending on your local authority, either a neighbourhood-based social worker or a multi-agency assessment team member (sometimes referred to as a MASH team) will offer a further assessment, immediate assistance or an assessment team signpost to appropriate community-based support and services.

Day care centres are local and help families with daily respite, but many of these have now closed.

Memory cafes are becoming more prevalent, and these are usually a good source of information and help. Usually in a town centre so easily accessible.

You can apply for a needs assessment to be carried out by social services. A health and social care assessment is carried out by social services to find out what help and support you need - like healthcare, equipment, help in your home or residential care.

Care plans and means tests are the first route which social services go down and they do everything to try and maintain independence and keep the person at home

When I first arranged for carers to come into his home three times a day for my dad, which we were privately funding as dad was over the savings/income threshold, there was a list of things that had to be done prior to them coming in, these are as follows:

All appliances in the house had to be safety checked for the safety of their care workers.

A key lock had to be installed outside so the carers could get in.

The house had to have smoke alarms and carbon monoxide alarms.

I had to arrange boiler and gas safety checks were up to date, for the carers' Health & Safety.

Safety equipment had to be installed in the shower ensuring it had grab rails and non-slip mats available, also a seat.

The hardest thing I had to think about was whether dad needed a DNR (Do Not Resuscitate) if he fell, had a heart attack or a stroke whilst they were caring for him. I had to call the GP and have a discussion with them and with dad. Dad was very matter of fact which made it easier for me and the doctor, and one was set in place.

The next Biggy for me was shopping for snacks and meals. As he was on his own, I arranged for 'Wiltshire Foods' which need only to be microwaved from frozen. They deliver and put them in the freezer for you and I found them to be good. (I am sure there must be other companies that do this or you can arrange Meals on Wheels to deliver if in they are in your area). Many local care homes also run a hot meal service either for collection or delivery. Although meal delivery was in place, I also had to do regular shopping for milk, bread, incidentals for sandwiches, and snacks, plus jellies and custards.

'This is me': these are forms to help carers and doctors to understand the likes and dislikes of the individual. i.e. tea or coffee, sugar or not, and including family members' names. These forms help if the person becomes upset, and should give ideas and topics or hobbies they are/were interested in to help conversation flow.

'This is me', should be filled in by the individual(s) who know the person best and, wherever possible, with the person involved. It is not a medical document.

Another useful tool could be a picture frame - large or small or more than one - in which you put photos from their life, picture of relatives and friends who might visit, identify the people, relative or friend and label the photos. This helps carers and visitors alike to find a common theme to talk about and help recapture memories.

Visitors could also bring their own letters from the past and additional photos.

Another route I thought of but did not follow up was getting a private 24-hour carer so they were known to him, but this can work out expensive and would need at least 3 to cover the week. Many do go down this avenue.

Chapter 3

Lasting Power of Attorney (LPA)

If you feel dementia or any long-term illness is happening to your loved one or yourself, I highly recommend that you arrange to put in place a Lasting Power of Attorney as soon as possible. They are as important as a will! These papers are legal documents which allow you or someone chosen by you to represent you in all things i.e. talk to a doctor, talk about treatment plans, deal with all banking, pay bills. The paperwork once signed and legalised allows your delegated attorney to act on your behalf, and in a worst-case scenario to make decisions on your behalf. Without one of these legal documents, even your close family cannot make decisions and cannot act on your behalf. Persuade them to do this as soon as possible where they will need help with their health or affairs.

There are two types of LPAs which need to be made, one for Health and Welfare and the other for Property and Financial affairs. Most people opt for the second one, but I cannot stress enough the importance of both. Without either you do not have the legal right to represent the person. If thinking of making an LPA please do both. In both forms, put as much information as possible, in health and welfare, your thoughts if you become infirm, what would you like done, would you make a living will, mention your thoughts on this, would you like to be resuscitated, if not say so. I appreciate it all sounds gloomy, but it makes life easier for those trying to look after your interests and saves so much soul searching for them. Maybe make an advance statement: you write this yourself with help if necessary, how you would like to be treated and any wishes you might have, i.e. dog care, like the light left on at night. This is not legally binding but must be taken into account. Or you can make an advance decision which is a living will which is legally binding.

https://www.gov.uk/power-of-attorney

Above is the legal site to download the papers from or do it online. You do not need to hire an expensive solicitor to fill them in. You can do it yourself or do it jointly with whoever needs the LPAs. some health visitors well help, others not. Work systematically through the papers and fill in and follow the instructions, it is very doable. As above put in as much information as possible. Now they do it online, but it can still be done by printing out the paper version.

The word attorney confused me, sounds so legal, but all it really means is who do you wish to act on your behalf, who in the long run do you trust enough to make all your decisions and oversee your life.

You can choose one or more people to be your attorney. If you appoint more than one, you must decide whether they'll make decisions separately or together. On the form there are 3 options to choose from:

1. Jointly – the 2 attorneys you select must make all decisions together. Choose people you trust to make your decisions.

2. Jointly and severally – this is one my dad chose, so all important decisions can be made by either attorney. It can cause issues if one attorney undoes the other attorneys' decisions, but hopefully you are both working in the person's best interest. This is a very important decision - will they get on, will they agree? Can you foresee trouble in the future? For me it was myself and my dad's second wife who had both been made attorneys' jointly or severally, but unfortunately, we did not get on. At first it did appear that this would not be an issue but further on down the line there were huge decisions to be made, who makes them, who receives the mail, all which can make life much harder than it needs to be. This can also lead to cost later on down the line if one or other needs to be removed or wishes to revoke being an attorney and the Court of Protection needs to be involved.

3. Jointly for some decisions and jointly and severally for other decisions. If this box is ticked a big explanation is required, and you

will have to write down all your choices on what your wishes are.

As a daughter I had no rights. So with GDPR and data protection it might now be worse for not sharing information, so an LPA is needed for each and every action tried to do on his behalf. Also, as an unmarried partner you will have no rights, even if been together 20years. So please arrange LPA's.

Taking care of their finances, paying bills, sorting out services electric, gas, telephone, renting or selling the home - all need a copy of the Lasting Power of Attorney.

To discuss the patient with a doctor, a social worker, a nursing home, you need one, or they will not share information.

The other hard question is finding a non-family member to declare you of sound mind, as many have lost touch with friends but hopefully not, also we found many do not wish to put a signature to their statement with the law as it is.

Once the LPA forms are filled in and all signatures gained, they need to be registered with the Office of the Public Guardians. This has a charge of £82 per Lasting Power of Attorney (2019). There are exemptions if you earn less than £12,000 or are on income support, then it is half price. If you choose a solicitor or specialist expect to pay approx. £450.00 each.

The LPA is only valid whilst the individual is alive. Then the Will takes over with the executor making the decisions.

Chapter 4

Court of Protection - part of the high court

The Court of Protection is a specialist family court, part of the High Court, which deals with all issues relating to people who lack the mental capacity to make specific decisions. A person may lack the capacity to make their own decisions for reasons including a physical or mental illness, a learning disability, a stroke or a brain injury following an accident and of course dementia.

If a person lacks capacity, it is this court who will make decisions on the way forward, if no Lasting Power of Attorney has been set up.
Firstly, a need will be to establish whether a person has capacity to make a particular decision, this will depend on doctors' reports, usually more than once.

Whether an action to be taken is in a person's best interests.
Whether a person is being deprived of their liberty, a form will be needed.

The validity of lasting and enduring powers of attorney.

The appointment of deputies – who should be appointed as a deputy.

The removal of deputies or attorneys, individuals or their families and objecting to applications made where these are not deemed to be in their best interests.

Once it has been established that a person lacks mental capacity in relation to matters concerning their property and financial affairs and/or health and welfare, the Court of Protection may appoint a Deputy to make decisions on their behalf.

A deputyship application can be made in respect of property and financial affairs but also in respect of some aspects of health and welfare.

Where possible, the Court would prefer to appoint a family member or a close friend to act for the person who lacks capacity, provided it is in their best interests to do so. Alternatively, a professional adviser, such as a solicitor or accountant may be appointed. If none of the above are able then a member of the local authority's social services department or a panel deputy can be appointed by the Court.

This cost, and it is not free, comes out of the assets held by the person under protection.

If it needs to go to court the case will be held in law courts and it is part of the Law system. It is not a different department - solicitors, counsel and judges are still involved. A judge makes the final decisions, exactly the same as in criminal courts, but no crime has been committed. The only thing the judge will do is take into account the mental capacity of the person and will do everything in that person's best interest.

None of this is quick, it is a slow ponderous machine, with many legalities, many doctors' visits to establish mental capacity.

Chapter 5

Choosing a care home:

Before you decide that this is the correct course of action, I advise you write a list of why you think, at this moment in time, it is best for them to go into a care home and why you are making your decision. It helps focus the thoughts and to know what you are looking for. Keep the list. I say this as I have looked at the list I made many times since dad went into a home. Some days through guilt, others to ensure I did the correct thing,

When I made the very hard decision to put dad in a home, I made a list of why, which I have included below; hopefully it will help you. At the time I felt so inadequate and guilty that I could not cope with the illness of someone I loved.

Once the decision was made, finding a care home was an ordeal in itself. My advice is to:

Decide if you need a specialist unit, care home with nursing, or just residential. Once you have an idea what you think you need make sure and look for homes and check the homes, look on QCC (Quality Care Commission)

https://www.cqc.org.uk/help-advice/help-choosing-care-services

Services they regulate;

Care Homes

Hospitals

Services in your home

Doctors /GP's Dentists

Clinics

Community services

Mental health services

Search the website for homes in the area and read the reports.

QCC does inspections. They rate each establishment on the following criteria: safe; effective; caring; responsive; well led. Once these are graded it leads to from: Outstanding, Good, Needs improvement, Inadequate.

Personally, I would not go for anything unless it is Good or Outstanding.

If you can ask about the staff records, how many staff do they employ, staff turnover as all these lead to your loved one's comfort, they get to know the faces so they don't want strangers all the time.

Check out the size of room, what is supplied, whether you can make it a bit personal.

Look at as many homes as possible in the time frame, try to just turn up so you can see the home as it is, with no special effort made to impress you. Some I thought I would really like I did not; some were too large, some too modern, some too cluttered, some too dark, some too old fashioned, some needed a good clean and fumigating, as they smelt. Many had rooms upstairs so required lifts, no good for the infirm. Some were too chaotic, some had too many corridors so patients couldn't find their way to their room. Some have colour zone corridors for them.

Do they have sensory rooms? Do they do activities during the week, do they bring in animals, and try to keep the residents in touch with the world and stimulate them in things they can do. The question nobody likes to think about but must be thought about, do they look after them till they depart this world, as in my case I did not want to have to move dad again. It would be too upsetting.

This is my list for why I put my father in a home in case it helps you.

1. Keep him safe, he was alone most of the day and vulnerable to strangers.

2. More interaction with others, never alone, social activities rather than the TV.

3. Outside carers struggling to cope. Dad was getting argumentative as every day the carer was

someone different who he did not know or recognise.

4. Falling out of bed, not being able to get up, just falling as he moved. He fell out of bed nearly every night and I could not pick him up, I had to call others to help so all were getting disturbed sleep.

5. He would not get up in the morning, as he had no routine.

6. Would not go to bed, he stayed in a chair all night and this was not good for his health.

7. He often sat on the toilet for hours, all night in some cases, and I found him cold and not able to move.

8. Pressure sores on his bottom where he did not move for long periods of time.

9. His home was fairly remote and quiet so the risk of strangers turning up could be a risk. Also just providing the right ambient temperature with fire on, heating on, even with temperature control, he could be too hot or too cold.

10. Phone call hazards (the marketing calls leading to visits and possible parting with money).

11. GP saying his heart beat was irregular, new onset Atrial Fibrillation.

12. Trying to coordinate all carers, doctors, nurses, food, cleaning, whilst still having to work and do my own housework, etc.

Why I chose the home I did

Suitable location for everybody to visit, (even though they didn't) small specialist unit, friendly approachable staff, clean, colourful, resident cat and budgies, nice safe garden which they could access on their own and still be safe, the home tries to encourage activities and take residents out whilst they can. They provided a nice clean room with a television and en-suite, full time nursing care and end of life care. Visiting times were not limited.

Availability of the nice care home is an issue, a bit like dead man's shoes which is equally upsetting if you think too deep about it, but there might be a waiting list.

These are all grim things to think about, but once done it can be put to the back of the mind and enjoy the person once again.

Cost is obviously another factor, but I cover this in the next chapter.

Chapter 6

Money and funding

Paying for it all. How? Who Pays?

When does the NHS pay?

Bank matters.

How do you find out what accounts they have, where their pensions are held, where they keep their savings? Hopefully all this is easy to find, if not, and you cannot get any help from the person, it is a case of trawling through their paperwork and notifying all of the relevant companies, with accompanying LPA of course! Department of Work and Pensions for the state pensions and any Attendance allowance they might get.

I started up and have kept a hard-back blank writing note book which is totally for LPA use and in this note book I jotted down everything to do with my father's life, when I made phone calls, to whom, dates, to whom I spoke, all relevant details so it is easy to recall at a later date when you need it again.

The frustration of believing businesses will do as you asked will take its toll and you will need this book. You can email confirmation, send relevant paperwork and 3 months later they will ask for it all over again. Keep all paperwork, keep all emails, note on them when you did what and who you spoke to. I had to learn to count to 100 never mind 10, it is a valuable lesson in patience.

Banking is a really important area of being an LPA. I had his accounts put on my online banking as it made it so much easier to manage. If you spend any of the monies keep receipts or note what it was for, as you are responsible for the accounts for revenue purposes and other beneficiaries later on.

I cannot stress the importance of being organised enough, it will make your life so much easier especially if you are also executor of the Will (which I hope they have, if not try and get them to make one).

If there is a need to put a loved one in a home, very often you do not have a choice especially if you are reliant on council care because they have no savings. It still pays to look around as there are some great nursing homes with good carers. A top up may be necessary but hopefully their pension will cover this cost.

If they own a house the council will often allow a loan against it but on sale of the home they must pay the debt back to the council.

Attendance allowance is worth applying for.

Carers allowance if the family are taking care of the loved one at home.

A useful article to read is 'When does the NHS pay for care?' by the Alzheimer's society (link below)

This article is about NHS continuing healthcare and NHS funded nursing care. Both are forms of funding available to all if you meet the criteria set down. The Department of health have a public Information leaflet available - NHS continuing healthcare and NHS funded Nursing care.

In chapter 11 there are a couple of articles on this subject which are very relevant to funding dementia care.

There are numerous websites with advice but the best I found are Which and Age UK

https://www.which.co.uk/later-life-care/financing-care/care-home-finance/self-funding

https://www.ageuk.org.uk/information-advice/care/paying-for-care/paying-for-a-care-home

https://www.alzheimers.org.uk/sites/default/files/migrate/downloads/when_does_the_nhs_pay_for_care.pdf

Chapter 7

Clothing

This sounds so obvious, but I did not think about it until I was asked, firstly by carers and then at the home. If someone needs help dressing, thought must be given to the ease of putting clothes on and comfort.

Once carers are Involved or one is in a care home, the style of clothing must change. No buttons, zips or ties preferably. There are a couple of reasons for this - ease of changing the person if they need help dressing, and zips and buttons can dig into the flesh when sitting for long periods or not moving much. Recommended clothing is loose trousers with elasticated waists for both ladies and men. Polo shirts, or loose tops. Easy care fabrics or non-iron clothes are required. Jumpers which have long front openings rather than go over the head are easier for them or the carers to put on.

Dad seemed to live in track suit bottoms and polo shirts with front opening fleeces or jumpers as a layer. It's not much different for women really - blouses and shirts with buttons are not practical, elasticated skirts and trousers are good.

Clothes also seem to wear out much quicker as they are always in a boil wash, so they fade quickly and appear worn.

Name labelling of clothes is a must. This sounds obvious really, but I did not think of it at all, just took dad's clothes in and wondered where they were going (DUH!). Labels can be purchased as sew ins or Iron-on name labels in all sorts of designs. There are loads of companies on-line that provide this service and the turn round is very quick. Permanent marker pen (Sharpie) is also good on slippers, shoes hats, etc.

Slippers must have a back in them, no mules as they are a serious trip hazard. They are also very hard to label, and every time I visited dad, he had different slippers on, sometimes his, usually not.

It is also advisable to label blankets and cushions.

Chapter 8

Family

Everyone in the family reacts to the diagnosis of dementia/Alzheimer's in a different way. Some shut it out, in denial, some are ostriches and hide their head in the sand and go on as if nothing has changed. Some go into grief mode, weep and wail and act as if the patient is dying imminently. There is no right or wrong, we all handle grief, which is what it is, differently and can cope better or worse.

A range of feelings, including:

fear

guilt

denial

jealousy

resentment

frustration

anger

sadness

tension or stress

embarrassment

an overwhelming sense of responsibility

unwillingness to take responsibility

despair and hopelessness

- helplessness

In all honesty I think I felt all these emotions at different times.

Once your loved one is in the home, then comes the difficulty of visiting them.

How often should one go? Some visit every day, some never. If you do visit always enter as if you have no cares in the world. Even if you are sad about the situation put on a smile, as they pick up on the negativity. I used to chat about anything I could think of - the weather, family, world affairs.

There is no right or wrong, I tried to visit dad every week, which I still feel guilty for. It should, in my head, have been every other day, but with busy working lives and your own family it becomes too much. Me personally, would rather pop in for half an hour to an hour and be assured he is ok.

Some family members will never go visit them in a home, and the reasons are numerous.

Again, their opinion should be valued.

They cannot bear to see the person they love be like they are, they would rather remember them as they once were.

"I would not know what to say", "What would I talk about"

"I would get too upset", "What if they don't know me"

My brothers and his grandsons found it very difficult to visit, one brother never went to see him, the other very occasionally and struggled with his own emotions.

At first, I gave them a hard time because I needed to share with them, but now so many families are the same I feel a bit more compassionate about it and can see their reasoning. They both did visit him in hospital and although if you asked dad if he had seen them, he would say he had not had any visitors, he would then mention them and we could talk about some of the funny things we had done in life involving them. So, although they are not aware they have had visitors, somewhere in the deep conscious mind they are aware.

I made up a photo album of his life from baby to present day and attempted to put pictures of friends and family and all the different locations he had lived. I also did a memory board for his wall and labelled it for talking points and to encourage conversation.

I think it is a mix of it all. All the points are valid, I feel all of them but always think if it was me in that position, I would still like to see a friendly family face. Hopefully they would know it was me but if not, they would still know I was special to them and be pleased to see me. Dad often did not know it was me, but he knew I was family and smiled.

One time when he had to go to hospital as he had fallen out of bed and he was in such pain they thought he had broken his hip. I rushed to the care home and went with him in the ambulance, so glad I did.

He was so confused, knew he was in hospital but did not know why, first the ambulance was fine, but waiting to see a doctor all dad kept saying was "I'm so glad you're with me." We were there all day with x-rays etc, and all that time Dad could not have a drink, as his Alzheimer's was quite advanced he needed thickener in his drinks and could not eat food as he would choke or spend for ever chewing. As A&E do not have this in the area, he could not even have water. If I ran off to get a drink, I always made him guard my handbag on his chest so they knew someone was with him and not to rush him off somewhere. We had a good giggle about it. I found this day although upsetting, sad, and worrying, very enriching. My dad and I were very close that day.

One of the hardest things I personally found to deal with and made me choke up and really hurt my chest, was feeding him. I arrived at a meal time and the carer said I could do it if I did not mind, I had not even taken on board he was being fed. The last people I had fed were my own sons and it just felt so wrong, it was just like feeding a toddler, he opened his mouth (but luckily, he did not spit it back) and shook his head when he had enough. I got used to it and felt it was a sign of caring, but that first time, I went home and sobbed.

Since that first visit to hospital dad went on to fall again, on a Monday morning. I met him at A&E this time. After a six hour wait, as they were so busy, they finally diagnosed that he had broken his hip! A&E had taken huge strides to help with dementia, all patients with it had a forget me not flower symbol on their stretchers. I was still afraid to leave him though, in case decisions had to be made. Then we were into a different place, he was taken to the ward where all signs of 'forget me not' vanished and he was treated as a competent adult. In some ways this is correct, but all it does in my view is to confuse as my dad could not understand. When the registrar asked him if he knew where he was he said yes, but follow that up and he said he was in Spain. Pain is another, are you in pain, he always said No, because he was sat and not in pain at that moment they asked him, but if he moved he was in agony. All a big learning curve.

All the individuals within the hospital were lovely and caring, but somewhere along the way compassion and caring is lost. No time, no money, too few staff. The arguments could be endless and this is not the place, but I do think that for any dementia sufferer without someone to fight their corner in the system it must be a confusing nightmare. My dad lost 4 Kg in this time as they gave him the food and then took it away. They put it out of sight or out of reach and a person with dementia will forget the food is there.

Chapter 9

Assistive technology

These are some ideas to help in the early stages and encourage independence using technology.

There are many gadgets, apps and ideas out there that could help. Please find below, some might not be helpful, some you might be able to adapt.

- Clocks

These can be habit from a lifetime of getting up, so a good idea as most people need some kind of alarm in the morning. Alarm clocks can also be used to remind you of appointments or events, or as a trigger to remind you that you need to take a pill or eat something. There are clocks on the market to tell night from day, others have all this and day, month and date. All helps confusion as they lose touch with the process of time.

- Put up a Noticeboard

Putting up a noticeboard in an obvious spot in your house can act as a trigger for memories. You could put it in the kitchen or by the front door to remind you to do things or take things with you if you leave the house. Noticeboards can also be useful for putting up a daily plan or a list of activities that you might want to do. Magnetic whiteboards are good because you can fix paper to them, write on them and wipe clean. Could be a blackboard, wipe board or cork board

- Sticky notes and labels

If a notice board is not possible, perhaps an alternative could be a post-it by the front door or labels on the cupboards. everybody relies on a certain amount of notes and labels to help them remember. It can make life a lot smoother and easier if you know exactly where you keep certain items by putting labels up. So, whether it's a note to remind you to put the bins out before you go to bed, or a sign to remind you where you keep your keys, they can be very useful

- Pill dispensers

If you need to take regular medication but have trouble remembering when you last took it, or even remember taking it at a certain time. Pills can be divided up into days, morning and evening and fitted into their own compartments. A family member often sorts the pills into a weekly dispenser, and now you can buy pill dispensers with a built-in alarm. An alarm will sound when you need to take your pills. Some dispensers are very high-tech and can be programmed to only release the set number of pills each time, locking away the rest of them until they're needed. The only problem is you need to remember what the alarm is telling you to do. (available from live better)

- Locator devices

If you keep losing your keys or glasses? You can attach special key rings to items which contain a <u>tracking device</u> that will beep if you press the corresponding colour-coded button on a base handset.

If you have a family member who likes walking but could get lost there are a few ideas: tracking devices, same as 'find my phone' app tracking; just ensure the phone is on their person. Also, door sensors can remind the person when they leave the house with a message to set off phone or, tell someone they are going out. And there are perimeter sensors which can be traced by a loved one. These are all options that are out therc.

- Talking memo pens or watches

Ideal for helping you to remember short shopping lists or a friend's phone number, memo watches let you record verbal messages, which means you can make a note of important bits of information and play them back when you need them. A talking memo pen acts in the same way. There are many apps, to use on phones, iPad or laptops. There are also many Alzheimer's memory games.

Sea Hero Quest is a game but whilst you are playing it you are part of research for the Alzheimer's Association. www.seaheroquest.com

Apps

Apps that you can get on your phone, iPad and other technology are listed below and might help if one is into apps. They might help in various aspects of coping, with all aspects of dementia. There will be other apps out there - these are a few I have found. These are not necessarily for the one with dementia but could help the carer.

- SAM App – SAM is an application to help you understand and manage anxiety.
- Mood Tracker – get daily insights into your ups and downs and spot patterns in your mood and behaviour.
- Happify – overcome stress and negative thoughts.
- Super Better – playing SuperBetter unlocks heroic potential to overcome tough situations and achieve goals that matter most.
- Mood Pixel – a minimalistic app that keeps track of your emotions, moods, thoughts and general well-being.

Meditation

- Buddhify – meditation app designed to fit into a busy modern lifestyle.
- Calm – 100+ guided meditations to help you manage anxiety, lower stress and sleep better.

NHS approved apps

- Big White Wall – an online community for people who are stressed, anxious or feeling low.
- Health and fitness trackers – from lowering blood pressure and cholesterol to tackling obesity and smoking, digital technology is transforming the way you can manage and improve your health.
- My Possible Self – take control of your thoughts, feelings and behaviour with the My Possible Self mental health app

Sleep

- Sleep Cycle – Sleep Cycle analyses your sleep and wakes you up at the most perfect time, feeling rested.

Confidence and self-esteem

- Build Confidence – put on your headphones and drift to sleep with this relaxing guided meditation intended to clear your mind and build your self-confidence.

Money management

- Expense Log – Expense Log provides a quick, easy and flexible way to track your expenses and incomes so you can see where your money is going or coming in.
- Acasa – all your bills in one app, hassle free.
- The Money Charity Budget Builder – a free, easy-to-use, interactive tool, available on desktop and mobile, which will help you create your own customised budget and then use it to keep track of your day-to-day spending.
- mySupermarket – supermarket price comparison tool.
- Plum – save more, invest in things that matter and reduce those pesky bills.

Time management

- Evernote – take notes anywhere, find information faster and share ideas with anyone
- Productive – Habit Tracker a tool that helps you build a routine of positive, life changing habits. Set personal goals, track your progress, and motivate yourself.

Exercise and nutrition

- <u>Couch to 5k</u> – the app builds you up gradually with a mix of running and walking.
- <u>One You Easy Meals</u> – a great way to eat foods that are healthier for you. You'll find delicious, easy meal ideas to get you going if you're ever short of inspiration.
- <u>https://findmyiphone.tips/download/</u>

Films and books, I recommend to help see dementia from their point of view.

Still Alice – (2015) Julianne Moore and Kristen Stewart – loved this film about early onset dementia, also, a book and stage play

The Notebook – (2004) an old one but all about love. Good one.

Elizabeth is missing. BBC (2019)

What they Had – with Hilary Swank (2018)

Alive inside – documentary about love of music and help music can bring if they enjoyed music previously. I did not like the film but loved the message

Friends with benefits – (2011) Justin Timberlake , a most unlikely film to leave a lasting message about dementia which it touches on, there is one part of the film when Richard Jenkins (the father) removes his trousers and everyone is embarrassed, but finally the son joins him. This part of the film changed my attitude to taking dad out when he was a bit pungent, made me take him out and not be ashamed of him but proud.

Contented dementia (book)

A year on Planet Alzheimer by Carolyn Steele

Chapter 10

Funnies

- ❖ People with dementia live in a state of normal - in a care home a lady said "I'm fed up I cannot go home till 7 – there's no buses."

- ❖ One visit I went to see my dad, he was dozing next to another man who was or appeared to be sound asleep. He suddenly sat up looked straight at me and said "Have you wet your pants?" and then went back to sleep.

- ❖ He was drinking his soup, I asked "What flavour?" he said it was nice cup of tea.

- ❖ After two years in the home, he was content, but once when I sat with him by his side, another lady resident called me a blonde cow, I think she thought dad was her husband and I had designs on him! So funny.

- ❖ On Christmas day 2017 we had dad for in my house for the day. He could not wash or find the toilet and did not move much, but slowly we noticed he was getting drunk, so we took more notice and realised that he kept going into the other room and finding the wine box, he could remember that, and was filling up his glass. He was happy that's all that counts!

❖ In the care home a rather large lady came visiting another resident and he said to her "You must eat a lot."

❖ Another time one of the care workers was shaving his face in the bath, he said to her "I feel sorry for your husband, tell him you like to torture old men" she laughed that the razor was blunt. I bought him a new razor and an electric one just in case.

❖ In a previous time when we were trying to care for him in his own home, my son and partner were there and had put him to bed, and were sat quietly in the front room waiting my arrival as I had been called away for some reason. Normally he needed help to move, but this evening, (my son called him a ninja) he moved with stealth and speed, next thing he was stood at the door. Surprises never cease.

❖ Again in the care home, they bought him a birthday present, it was all wrapped up in wrapping paper and they asked what he hoped it was, "I hope it is a tyre pump, I need one", no it was a hat!

- In hospital he was convinced there was a rabbit under the bed.

Please find the humour in all they say, once they have passed on you will appreciate those times.

Chapter 11 - Miscellaneous

Hope for the future

A drug designed to reverse the everyday forgetfulness that sets in at middle age will soon be entering clinical trials on humans.

https://www.dailymail.co.uk/health/article-6705369/New-drug-reverses-memory-loss-aging-set-human-trials.html

A free-to-use iPad based tool, the app has been developed using human factors testing to reduce the error rate when used in routine clinical practice.

https://www.plymouth.ac.uk/news/dementia-screening-app-wins-national-award

And they also claim the results could explain why the trials treating all patients with the same drugs often prove unsuccessful.

https://www.dailymail.co.uk/health/article-6463417/Alzheimers-NOT-one-disease-Sci...entists-group-memory-robbing-disorder-six-categories.html

A novel attempt at taking dementia sufferers back to the good old days into which their dimming minds have so often retreated.

https://www.theguardian.com/society/2018/oct/05/nursing-home-lets-people-with-dementia-live-down-memory-lane

Dementia Tests

https://www.psycom.net/dementia-test/

https://www.nhs.uk/conditions/dementia/diagnosis-tests/

https://www.nhs.uk/news/neurology/study-examines-quick-and-simple-dementia-test/

Articles in Press

A personal story about labelling photos

https://www.theguardian.com/society/2018/oct/31/she-is-looking-for-memories-love-after-dementia-photo-essay

https://www.dailymail.co.uk/tvshowbiz/article-6642397/Dame-Barbara-Windsor-requires-24-hour-nursing-care-battle-Alzheimers-worsens.html

someone is diagnosed every 3 seconds.

https://www.bbc.com/news/health-48094398

18/12/2019

https://www.dailymail.co.uk/news/article-7807573/Two-MILLION-/Britons-forced-care-family-member-dementia.html

Views on Dementia in the media

Daily mail 3.10.18

Of all the diseases of old age, dementia is perhaps the cruellest.

And for whatever reason — longevity, lifestyle, pollution, genes, we don't really know — more and more people are facing the spectre of terminal cognitive decline.

In the UK, there are currently around 850,000 people suffering from dementia in one form or another.

By 2025, they will number more than a million. One person develops the disease every three minutes. It's heart-breaking.

But what's even more distressing is the way those with dementia, and the relatives who inevitably care for them, are treated.

Second-class citizens doesn't quite cover it. Cattle class, more like.

This week the plight of sufferers was brought into sharp relief by research from the Alzheimer's Society, showing that individuals diagnosed with this illness face a 'dementia premium' on their care home costs.

That means anything from £33,000 to £62,000 a year compared with £26,00 to £41,000 for standard care.

This alone would be bad enough. But if you consider the fact that dementia patients are expected to pay for their own care, unlike say, someone suffering from heart disease, diabetes or cancer and the whole sorry situation adds up to a cruel kick in the dentures, especially when you also consider that even with the average house price in the UK being around £220,000, selling a treasured family home, one that you have laboured a lifetime for, isn't going to buy more than a few years of respite.

As if suffering from one of the cruellest diseases known to mankind wasn't bad enough, as if being robbed of your mind wasn't humiliation enough, we'll also make you sell your home to pay for it.

And then charge you through the nose for the privilege.

Surely I cannot be alone in feeling furious at the injustice of it all. These are some of the most vulnerable people in our society.

Yet they are effectively being mugged, on a daily basis and in plain sight, and no one seems to care.

Certainly not the self-appointed social justice campaigners of Twitter, or the virtue-signalling luvvies of stage and screen.

Not the politicians, more interested in arguing over power than worrying about people who might not be around come the next election, or the BBC, too busy espousing more fashionable causes such as Black History Month or #metoo.

Adding insult to injury is the fact that, unlike so many of those who place intolerable pressure on the system, dementia sufferers are, by the very nature of their advanced years, one of the few groups of people who have actually contributed to the NHS materially.

Through a lifetime of taxation and National Insurance contributions, they have paid their dues.

Only to be told, in their time of need: sorry, there's none left. And all because they happen to be suffering from the wrong disease.

What bitter irony for sufferers and their families to watch, powerless, as the Government extends costly treatment to the world and his wife (sometimes literally) while refusing to provide vital assistance to those who have supported it the most.

I'm not arguing that dementia patients should have special treatment. Merely that they should be treated like any other group of people suffering from a major life-changing condition. On the NHS.

The very least they deserve is freedom from the stress of financial worry.

To be allowed to spend what little quality of life they have left in the comfort of familiar surroundings, in their own homes, not in the hands of strangers in institutions who see them not as people, parents, partners, loved ones, but as cash cows!

Daily mail on Tuesday 9 July 2019 £15 billion tax on dementia

Families have spent nearly £15 billion caring for relatives with dementia in the two years they have been waiting for ministers to reform social care, a report reveals today.

The Alzheimer's Society last night branded the system a 'tax on dementia'.

A Government green paper – which ministers promise will fix England's broken care system – has been delayed six times since it was commissioned in March 2017. Meanwhile, the middle classes have borne the brunt of the cost of dementia support, with families denied the chance to hand their homes to their children.

The Alzheimer's Society demanded an immediate cash boost to help families survive while ministers come up with a long-term solution to the crisis.

Anyone with more than £23,250 in assets – including the value of their home – has to pay the full cost of their care, which can reach £100,000 a year. Many have to sell their house or re-mortgage.

The Government – which has spent £9.3 billion on dementia care in the past two years compared to the £14.7 billion paid by families – said only that the green paper will be published at the 'earliest opportunity'.

It is just the latest in 20 years of Government commissions, reviews and proposals to deal with the social care crisis. All have been shelved or abandoned because of the eye-watering figures involved.

The new numbers, compiled by the society, shine a harsh light on the divide between medical care, which is provided free for all by the NHS, and social care, which is paid for by anyone with savings.

The society said this means a 'gross inequity' whereby someone diagnosed with cancer has their bills met, while someone with dementia – for which there are no effective medical treatments – faces financial ruin.

More than 850,000 people in the UK have dementia – a number that has grown by 33,000 in the past two years.

The society calculated that since the social care green paper was announced in the 2017 Budget, people with dementia have spent more than a million unnecessary days stuck in hospital beds, despite being well enough to go home, at a cost to the NHS of more than £340 million.

Society chief executive Jeremy Hughes said: "The human cost of the delays to the social care green paper is appalling".

The longer we wait, the more people with dementia are left to struggle with a dreadfully broken system, forced to spend their life savings and sell their possessions to pay for the catastrophic costs of care.

"This tax on dementia – which sees people typically spending £100,000 on care bills – is cruel and unfair. And the amount and quality of care they're getting for it – those who can afford it – just isn't good enough."

Mr Hughes called for the creation of a £2.4 billion interim fund for dementia support, adding: "Hundreds of thousands of people affected by dementia in this country are facing financial punishment, just because they happened to develop dementia and not some other disease".

"The evidence of the gross inequity continues to pile up, and yet still the Government does nothing."

Health Secretary Matt Hancock has admitted the current system is unsustainable and unfair – and just last week Defence Secretary Penny Mordaunt conceded it was 'fair criticism' to say the Government had kept the public waiting too long.

But the green paper – which is understood to have at its heart a state-backed insurance scheme – has been held up for at least a year by wrangling between Downing Street and the Treasury over costs.

Mr Hancock said last month: "The sign of a civilised society is how we treat the most vulnerable and our social care system is not up to scratch."

Barbara Keeley, Labour's shadow minister for social care, said: "This research reveals the shocking scale of the social care funding crisis. The continued inaction on social care funding from this Government is taking a heavy toll on the finances of people with dementia and their families."

17/7/19

Dementia care - your fury: Unlike other illnesses, sufferers of dementia who saved all their lives pay for their care AND subsidise others - and as your outraged letters show, it's a cruel injustice that MUST now end

By DAILY MAIL READERS
PUBLISHED: 23:47, 16 July 2019 | UPDATED: 07:25, 17 July 2019

Following new figures showing an increase in the number of people suffering from dementia, the Mail's Sarah Vine wrote movingly about how our broken care system is bankrupting hard-working families. She argued it was totally unfair that, even though dementia is a medical condition, unlike other diseases its sufferers and their families have to foot care costs. Her words struck such a chord with Mail readers so infuriated by the scandalous cost of caring for their loved-ones that they wrote to us in their hundreds. Here we present just a small selection of your letters...

THE WRONG PRIORITIES

My wife's dementia care has cost us £50,000 per year since 2008. Given the government manages to find billions for vanity projects like HS2, funding a decent care system shouldn't be a problem. BRIAN HENDY, Romsey, Hampshire.

My father-in-law fought in D-Day and later served for 30 years in the police force. His one ambition was to own a house, which he eventually achieved after many years. But as he grew old, he was admitted to a care home with dementia. Their very modest savings were soon exhausted and they had to sell their beloved home. Surely our elderly deserve better than this? JB, address supplied.

HEEDING BAD ADVICE

My mother is 87 years old and has only made one big mistake in her life: to heed the advice of the State and save for her old age. She didn't drink, didn't smoke and was frugal with her earnings.

But three years ago she was diagnosed with dementia and is now paying nearly £1,000 per week in care.

The mental anguish this has caused her is nothing short of a scandal. SD, Epsom, Surrey.

After my father died when I was a child, my mother worked seven days a week to keep a roof over our heads. She eventually saved up for a home, but never had anything else. But now that she has dementia, we have had to put her beloved house on the market to pay for her care. We have done everything right in our lives but are still the losers. CP, St Albans, Herts.

My wife was diagnosed with Alzheimer's in early 2006 and I cared for her at home until I had to seek professional help in 2011. It was the worst decision I have ever had to make.

She passed away in 2016, after we had paid £121,276.16 in fees — while a friend's mother, who had no savings, paid nothing.

Where's the justice in that? TM, Stanton, Suffolk.

MUM'S HOME WILL GO TOO

My mother was diagnosed with dementia about eight years ago and lived with me for over five years. But it became too much and we had to put her in a care home.

I understand that there has to be a line somewhere, but because my parents were diligent with their finances, she does not creep under the £23,000 threshold. All they worked so hard for is now being ploughed into her care — and eventually her home will have to go. Vannessa, Taunton, Somerset.

We are left to struggle. I have tried three times to get nursing care for my dear wife — only to be told that her needs were insufficient. I have now paid over £100,000 for my wife's care — and some have paid a great deal more! DB, Warrington, Cheshire.

For years I acted as the main carer for my wife who has Alzheimer's. But in 2016 I fell on the staircase, injured my back and broke my ribs. At that point, my daughter stepped in and secured my wife a place in a care home. This September will mark three years since we started paying for her care, while others have been supported by the care system. How is that fair? RS, Draycott. Derbyshire.

In 2011, my father had a stroke and was in hospital for three months, where it became clear he was also suffering from vascular dementia. He moved into a care home and by the time he died four years later, had incurred costs of £126,000. This is totally unacceptable. GB, Hampshire.

ALZHEIMER'S VICTIM

My husband had Alzheimer's and was in care from December 2016 to March 2018. His care costs during this period totalled £75,670. J.G., Bagshot, Surrey.

My mother is 98 and has needed dementia care for the last four years. She has had to pay £150,000 so far and is running out of cash. What really galls me is that politicians and civil servants, with their gold-plated salaries and pensions, constantly ignore this desperate situation. JANE F, London.

USEFUL WEB PAGES

https://www.gov.uk

Government website

http://www.ageuk.org.uk/

Age UK: - 08001692081 – leading charity for old people with good advice and help

https://dementia.livebetterwith.com/

- a helpful site with aides and advice

www.alzheimers.org.uk

This is the leading charity for those with dementia or Alzheimer's – 020 7423 3500

National Dementia Helpline on 0300 222 11 22

https://www.theguardian.com/money/2015/jan/31/lasting-power-attorney-planning-unexpected

https://www.theguardian.com/lifeandstyle/series/doing-it-for-dad

If you like statistics

https://www.alz.co.uk/research/statistics

https://www.respectprocess.org.uk/patietsandcarers.php

https://www.nhs.uk/conditions/end-of-life-care/

https://medical-dictionary.thefreedictionary.com/dementia

CHAPTER 12 – Mon Vie

'Mon Vie' is the start of dads' life written in his own words, it just stops but is still interesting. How life is so different now to then.

I was born at Railway Cottage in Pontypool, South Wales, my mother, being welsh. My father was a house builder from Bristol and very soon my mother took me home to Bristol. One of my earliest memories is of the day when Dad sold his pony, Daisy, which was about the time that we moved to No 64, Sandgate Road, Brislington, in 1934. He liked his pony and trap, but Daisy didn't like the camber of the road and persisted in using the crown, which was becoming a nuisance with the increase of motor vehicles, a big joke when you think of the mass of traffic today. We were then without transport for a few years. Life at Sandgate Road was very pleasant for my sister 3 years my senior and myself. We had a large paved area in an enclosed, very private garden complete with swinging boat for two. On my 8th birthday I was given my first two wheeled bike, which I quickly learned to ride and from then on I was very independent. My best friend, Alfie, had no bike, so he and I would travel miles, with him running alongside until he was tired, then we would swop over for a while.

At Xmas we always travelled by train to Pontypool to stay with Mum's sister, Aunt Glad, Uncle Joe and cousins Ray & Elsie. There was also cousins May, married to Arthur living a few doors away and Dorothy, also married and living at Griffithstown, 4 miles away. It always seemed a magic time to me. Their house, a standard three-bedroom terrace, with toilet down the garden, seemed to be filled with people all through the Xmas. Aunt Glad kept open house and the table would be full of food from morn till night. The front door was open and there seemed to be a continuous stream of people calling in to convey Xmas Greetings, enjoy a glass of homemade wine and partake of some food. I remember one day when a man came in, greeted everyone, helped himself to some food and enjoyed a glass of wine, before thanking Aunt Glad and leaving. Aunt Glad then turned to Joe and said "Who was that?". Joe said "I don't know, I thought he was a friend of Arthur's". Arthur said "I have never seen him before" and we never found out who he was!. Xmas morning

Uncle Joe would take us for a walk up the mountain, usually in deep snow, leaving Aunt

Glad and May to cook Xmas lunch over the hot coals on their open Kitchen Range and we always ate very well. I well remember one Xmas, I must have been aged 7 or 8, when I arrived there with a cold. That night I was sent to bed with a well-worn, smelly, 12 month old pack of goose grease on my chest.

Every year there would be a huge Goose ordered for Xmas, the thick layer of fat would be stripped from the carcase before cooking, wrapped up in clean muslin and put aside to deal with any colds during the following year. Following that experience, my biggest fear was to have a cold at Pontypool. It may have been the fear that kept me clear of colds at Xmas! Cousin May was prone to swear a lot, particularly when stressed and I recall one such morning when the doorbell rang. "That must be the bloody milkman" said May. Her 3 year old daughter heard her, ran to the door and greeted the milkman with "Are you the bloody milkman?". Xmas at Pontypool was always a highlight of the year and it continued all through the war years. It always amazed me how Aunt Glad managed to maintain such a good table, despite the rationing.

Few families at that time had transport and a great deal of our needs were purchased from street sellers, who arrived regularly every week with horse drawn wagons, butchers, bakers, fishmongers, greengrocers, grocers and others. Each one had their own signal of their arrival and were the regular meeting places for the gossip among the house wives, it being very rare at that time for a house wife to be out to work. Dad had his builders yard at the back of Alford Road, about one mile away, where he had bought land and was building several quality semi's. From the age of eight I used to spend as much time as I could up on the site, helping out by running errands, collecting nails, screws, etc. from the store and learning a lot about building in the process. Two of my uncles, worked for Dad and made me feel very useful. On Saturdays, pay day, I felt very grown up as I stood at the end of the queue of workmen for my six old pence pocket money.

The War Years

When war was declared on Germany in 1939, many things started to change. Rationing was started for many of the everyday groceries, clothes and of course petrol. There were suddenly a lot of cars on the market at reasonable prices and Dad bought his first car, a second hand Standard 8, complete with a trailer. He was able to get a reasonable allowance of petrol for his business, so we had transport all through the war. It was also about this time that we moved, a rambling three storey house of red sandstone, with large rooms and high ceilings and it was shortly after this that my younger sister Pat arrived. When the war started coal was rationed and fires were restricted to the living room, though occasionally when we had visitors we were allowed one in the large front room, so you tended to get rather hardy. I remember all the iron railings around the streets being taken away as metal was in short supply. It was not long before the blitz's started on

Bristol and we had a bomb hit our garden wall, doing a lot of damage, when the jerries tried to hit the engineering factory just behind us. We also had a landmine which had a direct hit on an Anderson shelter across the road, killing the whole family, including a friend of mine. It was then decided that I should be evacuated to South Wales to stay with relatives, my sister was already established at School, so she stayed at home.

All my schooling to date had been at Wick Road Junior, where I had followed in the wake of my sister, who was it seemed, very academic and I was regularly being told that I would never be as good as my sister. It had the opposite effect on me to that which was intended and I hated it. I soon settled into the quieter life style at Pontypool and into the school at Wainfelin with my cousin Ray. I liked my teacher from the start, he lived on his fathers farm and would regularly start the day with a little story about the animals, intuitively sensing when we were all primed ready to do some work. He encouraged me, persuaded me to take extra work home and soon had me reading Shakespeare. For the first time I began to appreciate that I did have a good brain up there. Life in Pontypool seemed very different to life in the big city of Bristol and a very short walk would take you up into the peace and quiet of the hills.
I had a friend, Bryn, whose father had a farm up in the hills and I used to spend a lot of time with Bryn on the farm at weekends. His father did a milk round with his horse and cart and when Bryn had finished his chores on the farm, we were allowed to ride the horse. We had no saddle and only a halter, so we

would get the horse alongside the five bar gate to climb on his back. The halter gave very little control as you could only steer him left, so a slap on his rump would send him careering around the field anti clockwise, whilst you hung on to his mane for dear life. In the holidays, I was farmed out to my other Aunts, presumably to give Aunt Glad a rest. At Aunt Olives, a spinster, I got to know Mum's Uncle Ben, a very fit mid 70's. He would often take me for long walks over the mountain to the next valley, a chunk of cheese with bread and lemonade for lunch at a Pub, before walking back. He believed in herbal cures and during the walk he would be collecting wild herbs to put in his rucksack. He always told me what they were for and how he would prepare them, but in one young ear and out of the other. How I wish I had remembered all that he taught me.

At that time in England one took the Scholarship exam at around 10 years to decide if you went to Grammar School or Secondary School, the higher your pass mark the higher the Grammar School. In Wales it was a little different, you had to decide which Grammar School you would try for, get it wrong and you could forfeit your right to any Grammar School. I was thinking of Abersychan Grammar, but my teacher persuaded me to go for West Mon High, the best school in South Wales and to the surprise of a number of people, I passed. I well remember the day when I visited the school with Mum to enrol, I was in heaven. It was a beautiful school, with every facility, swimming pool in the basement and my first lesson was to be latin! I could visualise myself being happy there. However, it was not to be and before my first term was due to start, we received a letter saying that it was with regret that I could not be accepted. As an evacuee I would be blocking the chance of a resident Welsh boy and I would have to return to Bristol, where I would be offered a Grammar School place. By this time it was getting near to start of term, most places having been allocated and Bristol could only offer me St George Grammar. It was not quite bottom, but not far short and a far cry from the standard of West Mon, what a let-down. I returned to Bristol and it was well into the first term when I reported to the school, September 1940.

Dad had promised me an adult bike if I passed the scholarship, but it was wartime and everything was scarce and I was living in hope. One day Dad came home and said "Your new bike is outside" I rushed out, only to see a heavy upright roadster, just like a policeman's bike, leaning against the wall. I was crestfallen and told Dad that I did not want a heavy bike like that, I wanted a sports bike. Dad tried to persuade me that it was a very strong bike that would last a lifetime, but eventually realized that I would not ride it. A few weeks later he came home with a second hand SUN sports cycle, with drop bars, which was much more to my liking and Dad started to use the roadster.

My introduction to the water

It was about this time that I joined the Sea Scouts, which, unknown to me at that time, was to considerably change the course of my life. It was a very active group, with a 27ft Montague Whaler in the

Bristol harbour and often on Sunday mornings a long string of scouts could have been seen cycling from Brislington to the harbour carrying a 17ft oar over one shoulder. I wonder what the police would have to say about that today? I well remember my first time out in the whaler, learning how to manage a 17ft oar and my struggle to toss it as we came alongside! The troop had only the funds which we raised ourselves, no sponsorships. We made regular trips with our handcart collecting jam jars from households, which we then delivered to the jam factory, for which we were paid half an old penny for each undamaged jar. The money was used to provide our very substantial camping gear and maintenance of our boats. Our 2 week summer camp was, in the early days at Highlittleton, some 10 miles out of Bristol, alongside a small wood, where we were allowed to chop wood for our fires and at the age of eleven I soon learned to swing a big felling axe safely, they believed in chucking you in the deep end in those days!. It was also close to a small stream, with a waterfall and deeper pool at the bottom, which was our regular washing place. For swimming we would walk some two miles to a deserted quarry where we romped about in the noddy in the deep ice cold water. I was at the camp in 1945 at the time of the Normandy landings. We heard a lot of planes going over and they were towing gliders. One of the gliders was in trouble as one of its tail fins came adrift and it was wallowing badly. The plane cast off the towline and the glider was disintegrating as it fell to earth approx. one mile from our camp. We all took off across the fields to see if we could help, but on arrival we found the remains on fire, with live ammunition firing in all directions. We lay down on the brow of the hill, watching as the local fire fighters tried to quell the blaze, but no one came out of the glider alive. We were a very subdued group of youngsters for the rest of the day.

I thoroughly enjoyed my scouting days, lapping up everything nautical and soon obtained my oarsman badge and went on for my Boatman badge (sailing), which led to a real highlight in my life. Our Skipper organised a trip on a 40ft deep sea sailing cutter in the Bristol Channel for six of the most qualified scouts. What a day that was, thrashing to windward with the spray flying and feeling the true power of the wind for the first time. It registered in my mind as a dream, but one which would affect my whole life and little did I think that I would eventually own an almost identical boat, except for being schooner rig.

We were also into canoeing as our skipper was a good friend of Percy Blandford, Scout commissioner and boat designer. A lot of kayaks were being built, using wood frame and canvas and we did a number of cruises down the rivers, Severn, Wye and Avon, carrying all our camping and other gear with us. I built three kayaks during my scouting days, a 14ft scout kayak, a 14ft PBK, (Percy Blandford Kayak) and in 1949 I built a PBK19 with my friend Collin Watson, specifically for an attempt on the Devizes to London Canoe record. The current holders had stopped for a sleep halfway, but we were confident that we could go straight through and carve a big slice off of their 65hr record. There were 72 locks to portage, so during the night when we had a long leg between locks, we took it in turns to lie down and have a kip in the bow while the other kept paddling. We set a new record of 53hours, but the following day Richmond Canoe Club came along with their lightweight racing canoes and knocked another 4 hours off

Our scout group regularly ran a Xmas Dance in the Church Hall and I particularly remember the one in 1945, when one of the older Girl Guides took me under her wing and taught me to dance Quickstep and Waltz. My sister Cynthia was a member of the YWCA of Park Street, Bristol, where they did ballroom dancing to live piano music once per week. She said they were short of men, so I went along with her and soon became a regular. I was the youngest there, though I was pretty tall and found I had plenty of partners. I learned fast, thoroughly enjoyed myself and very soon realized that it was the guys who were light on their feet and took to the floor who got the girls, while most of the guys propped the bar up.

In 1947 my sister, Cynthia, persuaded me to keep her company on a visit to a fortune teller. The lady was a wizened old dear, with makeup plastered on. She read my hand and told me that I would be a great traveller, spending a lot of time overseas, but would always return to England. At that time, few middle-class people holidayed out of England. She said "You are courting a tall, dark haired lady, but the lady you marry will be fair haired. She also told me that I would have a long healthy life, living to age 89, but with one spot of ill health on the way, all very hard to visualise at that time. (Strangely, all these foretelling's have come true.)

1946 was the year I sat for my School Certificate, I thought I did pretty well with several passes and a number of credits, however I failed at English language examination, which at that time was a compulsory subject and all my passes and credits counted for nothing. I was therefore a complete failure with no School Certificate. What a system? I had little respect for the school and even less for the batty English Teacher, so in my usual stubborn way refused to stay on for another year and do a resit. I had a good discussion with Dad concerning my future. I wanted to go to the school of Navigation at Monmouth to train as a Navigation Officer for the Merchant Navy and Dad was on the verge of agreeing to pay for my admission. However, the rest of his family, who had lost a brother at sea during the 1st World War, ganged up on me and I was eventually persuaded that I would do better to stay in the family business, building. Dad did not want me to follow him in his building business, preferring that I work on the professional side. I was good at mathematics and Quantity Surveying attracted me, particularly as it was a job where I would be spending a lot of time out of doors.

Dad arranged for me to be articled to a firm of Chartered Surveyors at Clifton in Bristol. This entailed the down payment of an agreed sum, in return for which I would work for no wages for 4 years whilst I was trained as a Quantity Surveyor. I therefore needed School Certificate or an equivalent to gain access to the Royal Institution of Chartered Surveyors, so I chose to study at home by correspondence course and sit the RICS entrance examination. I settled into my new job and persevered with studying at home. I was not very impressed with the amount of tuition that I was getting at the office and felt that I was being used as slave labour. Most of my time was spent squaring dimensions and general odd job man, until one day looking for some particular document I came across my Articles. I had a quick look and realized that they had never been ratified by the RICS.I talked to Dad and said that I thought that I could learn just as much as a Trainee Assistant and reckoned that I should break my articles. We saw the family Solicitor, who wanted to sue the firm of Surveyors, but Dad said no, as it would be bad start in my profession and just claimed refund of the fee.

1948 I started work with Jack Clegg, Quantity Surveyor, as a Trainee Assistant, earning 10 old shilling {50 new pence} per week. What a difference, I was chucked in the deep end in no time, and I loved it. I had by now passed the RICS Entrance exam and applied to take the RICS Exams, only to be told that Jack Clegg was not considered a suitable place of employment. Enquiries told me that Jack Clegg had had some arguments with the RICS in the past and had therefore been blacklisted. My attitude was "To hell with the RICS, I preferred to stay where I was learning plenty and I decided to join the Institute of Architects and Surveyors. I then arranged a correspondence course to prepare for their first exam, a decision that I would rue later.

My last year at Grammar School, 1946, found me doing a lot of miles riding with a friend and late that year he suggested that I have a go at racing in his Club 25 mile time trial the following Sunday. I rather fancied the idea, so we popped up to see the Secretary of the Bristol Road Club on the Friday evening, I joined the Club and rode in my very first race the following Sunday and the bug had bitten! In 1947 I had a full season of racing, taking every opportunity to compete at 20, 25 & 50 miles. In late September I had my first mention in the local paper when I rode the Bath CC 25 on a hard day with a time of 1.7.20, only 3 minutes behind the winner and came away with first handicap prize. I was still riding the Sun Sports bike with Endrick touring wheels, now getting a little rusty and had a mention in Cotter Pin's cycling news in the Evening Paper. He commented on my ride as a relative newcomer to the sport and wondered what I would be capable of if I had a decent bike. I showed it to my Dad and the outcome was that he and my Uncle Bill shared the cost of a new bike and I was able to order a hand built Holdworth, built to my own Specification for the following season. Wow, was I a happy bunny!

I had a pretty good season in 1948, Breaking the Club record for 30 miles in May, with 1.17.44., Second place in the WTTA 50 miles in June with 2.16.27. In July I rode my first 100 mile TT, finishing 11th on a very blustery day with 4.55.20 and set a new Club record for 25 mile with 1.3.1. I was finding that I had plenty of stamina and enjoyed the longer races, so August found me riding in my first 12 hr event, where a comfortable 224.75 miles gave me

5th place and with Club mates John Thomas and Den Smith we also took the team prize. In September I knocked a few more seconds off the Club 25 record with 1.2.55. I was beginning to feel my feet and getting known in the racing fraternity, so October saw me attempting to break R.C.Manning's Western Counties Road Record Association straight out 50 mile record of 2.2.15. My first attempt narrowly failed, but at second attempt on 24th October, pushing an 86" fixed gear (in those days very few riders used variable gears) I succeeded and brought the record under 2 hours with 1.59.14

Cycling was becoming my way of life, it gave me a wonderful feeling of freedom, there was a wonderful camaraderie and friendly rivalry between the Clubs and gave one a great feeling of belonging. Our weekend Club runs often included as many as 20 riders and even on the coldest winter days usually exceeded 100 miles. I set my heart on the national Best All Rounder competition, which was based on a riders average speed using their fastest 25, 50, 100 mile and 12 hour time trials of the season and I was packing in over 13,OOO miles per year on the bike. Quite often I would be out on the road by 0730 hrs, enjoying the freedom of the road, (much less traffic in those days, particularly on the B roads) and stopping only for breakfast, elevenses and lunch before meeting the Club for tea. I was not flush with cash, so I always carried 6 raw eggs which I could swallow down for quick energy and a pack of dates, which I could guarantee would be adequate to get me home if I ran out of cash. I was quite happy on my own, knowing that I would have company for tea when I was getting tired, but occasionally Phil & I would do a night ride, Saturday afternoon to Sunday evening, such as London & back, which clocked up some 250 miles. The social season was filled with the various Club Prize-giving's, Dinners/Dances and inter Club rendezvous for sing songs with piano at country pubs. Our Club got the nickname of the Black & Tan Wheelers due to a number of us drinking Guineas and Bitter.

1949 was a great year for me and looking back I just wonder how I fitted it all in, but I have no doubt that my studies did suffer. I started the season with Avon Rough Stuff, 19 miles across country, using farm tracks and one section carrying the bike a few hundred yards over rough terrain. Half a mile from the finish I crashed on a muddy bend, remounted feeling very bruised and finished third. A good start to the season in which I was rarely out of the frame (the first three). In March I felt honoured to be asked to do a demonstration sprint on rollers at the Bristol Health and Strength Show to be held on 6th May. I had never ridden on rollers and had visions of making a spectacle of myself as I came crashing off the rollers, on stage in front of hundreds of spectators. I was told that Charlie Rowatt in my club had a set of rollers and he agreed to lend them to me. I soon became proficient on them and on 6th M ay I was very happy with my first ever performance on stage. I was gaining confidence fast. On15th May I took second place in the WTTA 50 with 2.07.01 and In June I won the WTTA 100 with 4.26.02. I had been the first in the West of England to beat two hours for straight out 50 and now the first to beat four and half hours for 100 out & Home, so I wanted to be the first to beat 240 miles in 12 hours. I decided a ride in the 24 hour event I talked to, a veteran rider of my Club who had always been very encouraging for me. He said "A great idea, just do not stop at the first two sit-down feeds". I said "But that means non-stop for the first 206 miles". "Yes" he said "but you can do it".

I stepped up my training, but late June my plans went haywire. I was on my way home from a training ride in the Welsh Mountains, riding fixed wheel as I always did. I was descending a long hill between Forest of Dean and Gloucester, doing around 40mph, when my chain caught the end of the crank. Being fixed wheel the back wheel was pulled forward and locked solid. Amazingly I was OK, but the rear end telescoped and the bike was out of action. I then had a long walk to Lydney Station, carrying my bike, where I caught the train to Gloucester and then to Bristol. It was very late that night when I arrived at Temple Meads, Bristol, where I telephone my Dad to come and pick up me and my bike. I now had a major problem, I was in the middle of the season and no racing iron. I dropped the frame in for urgent repair, but was told that it would be several weeks minimum before I could expect it back. I was devastated, but my Dad and uncle Bill got together, they suggested that I needed a spare frame for such emergencies and they provided the cash for me to order a new hand-built frame from Granby to my specification. In the meantime, a good friend loaned me his spare bike, not tailored for me, but it tided me until my own frame was returned, luckily in time for the 24Hr. The Granby arrived a little later, a very rigid, short wheel based frame, which turned out to be great for the shorter events, but too rigid and too much vibration for long distance.

Mid July I set off on a 10 day tour of Devon & Cornwall with, a friend from Bristol South CC. We travelled light, no tent and both short on cash, so we slept rough most nights. Our first night, having set off after work Friday night, we travelled late and laid our sleeping bags on hardcore under a bridge, too tired to notice. At Seaton we settled down under a lean-to shed as the weather looked rather unsettled. It rained heavily during the night and unfortunately the wind veered, blowing straight in to our shelter, soaking our sleeping bags. Around dawn, Dennis & I were up, making a brew and trying to get warm, so we spent the next night at Salcombe Youth Hostel, hoping to dry our sleeping bags. We then had a variety of nights in the open, our most memorable being on Tintagel Point, under the stars on a fantastic night, with the surf pounding on the rocks below. We had a similar night on Hartland Point. All told we had a fabulous week, we ate well, we slept well most nights and we didn't spend a great deal.
August 7/8th found me riding in my first 24 hour event on a 77 inch fixed wheel. I took Charlies advice, I kept going, non-stop, till the third sit down feed, went into the lead and stayed there. Twice during the evening a Spectator waved a pint of beer at me, so I stopped and downed the pint in record time. I had a burst tyre and had to borrow a wheel from a spectator, then during the night a marshal, who I think was half asleep, misdirected me, as a result of which I did a further 3 miles off course which did not count. I covered four hundred and forty-five- and three-

quarter miles, 13 miles ahead of Jack Nunn, the scratch man. With John Thomas and Den Smith, we also took the team prize. The British record at the time was held by Gordon Basham with 453 miles. I then found that at age of 19, I was the youngest man to have won a 24 hour race, it having always being assumed as being a race for mature experienced riders. Charlie had passed on the benefits of his experience to me and I owed my success to him. I lost 14 lbs in weight during the race, 7 lbs returned in a week, but well into the social season before I recovered the other 7 lbs. Two weeks later I broke the Club 25 mile record again with I.0.27 on the Somerset flats on 86 inch fixed gear.

On 28th August, I achieved my wish, to be the first man to beat 240 miles in 12 Hrs in West of England, totalling 242 plus miles, despite feeling well below par in the latter stages. Unfortunately, Arthur Rich, starting 10 mins later than me finished 330 yds further up the road than I did, putting me into second place and taking the short lived record off me. No one had told me how close he was! The following evening I collapsed at home, with high temperature and sickness. I had food poisoning and later heard that many other riders had gone down with it. One of the pack of sandwiches handed up had contained dried egg, the war time replacement for eggs which were still short in supply. Dried egg did not keep well once mixed and cooked and our sandwiches had been prepared the previous day. I was much more wary of hand up feeds after that and often organised my own. I was very happy with my season as a whole and then I heard that I had another bonus. I received a certificate to say that I had achieved a position of 52nd in the British Best All Rounder Competition, which is based upon a riders best 50 m, 100m and 12 Hr in the whole of England.

1949 was not without its troubles. Late spring, I had joined my friend Colin on a week's holiday at Poole, staying at the local scout hall and boating with the Poole scouts. We took our canoe down by train and explored the vast Poole harbour. The scouts had an old lifeboat which a crowd of us took sailing, very safe but hardly exciting sailing. One day as I was standing on the thwart, making an adjustment to the sail, the helmsman allowed the boat to jibe, throwing me backward and bouncing the base of my spine on the steel keelbox. It was extremely painful and spoilt the rest of my week at Poole. A week after returning home found me on a weekend away in Somerset with the Road Club. From then on I was plagued with backache for the rest of the season and it got progressively worse. I was still riding but using the lower riding position less and less. Eventually I had to seek help and it was found that I had dislocated my pelvis, no doubt the fall in the sail boat! and had also badly strained my back muscles. Dad paid for me to have private treatment from an Osteopath to correct the displacement and then followed up with some massage treatment. The masseur, having heard my story, said "I am not surprised that you pulled your back, your legs are too strong for your body". The day before the 24hr race I went for a full body massage and it helped considerably. However, I rode most of the race using the top position on the bars to avoid over stressing my back. I gave the masseur's words a lot of thought and realized that I had 26" thighs and only a 30" expanded chest, completely out of proportion! I then wrote to the cycling Doctor who gave me an exercise routine to strengthen my back three times per day. This included toe touching, gradually increasing the repetitions and later suggested using some heavy books to increase the resistance. I progressed with the routine, gradually increasing the number of books.

I had a fabulous time during the social season in 1949, with a round of Club Dinners, collecting my many prizes and apart from my aching back. 3rd December, I met Barbara Spencer, who was the current fast 25 miles from Bristol South CC. She sure made an impression on me, so after a few dances together at the Club Dinner, we arranged to meet the following week and on 11th December I took her home for tea. Barbara was not a great Dancer, but she loved Opera, a love which she shared with her Dad. I suggested that we both go to Dance lessons together and I would give Opera a try. Opera came to the Bristol Theatres three, maybe four times per year and I did get to enjoy it, though I found some pretty heavy going! We went dancing every week and very soon got our Bronze for Ballroom and over the years progressed to Silver for Ballroom & Latin.

I had been given deferment to allow me to study, but if I failed an examination I would no doubt be called up. I did not fancy going into the Army, so in October 49 I joined the Royal Navy Volunteer Reserve in the hope that it would enable me to do my two years' service in the Navy. It entailed one evening per week aboard the Flying Fox, berthed in Bristol Harbour at Hotwells and I was to be trained as a Signaller. It was in some ways a follow on from my Sea Scouting days and my love of the water. I joined in with the Boxing Team, until I was advised that I would do better at Wrestling. I also represented the Bristol Branch in the RNVR Swimming Championship in London, coming third in the 400m freestyle. One year later I was thinking a little more sensibly, realizing that two years away from Quantity Surveying would take a bit of catching up. I therefore quit the RNVR December 1950 and decided to press for Royal Engineers when called up.

1950 was not a good season, sport wise. Getting fit again after the social season came particularly hard, as I was still suffering a great deal of backache. Barbara & I were spending every opportunity together, walking, rowing on the river at Saltford, evening trips to the Cinema, Theatres, dancing most Saturday nights and in July we took a trip on the Cambells Paddle Steamer to Barry Island across the Bristol Channel. However, I did try to keep four evenings per week clear for studying my correspondence course for my professional examinations. One of the requirements for the first examination was to complete a set of drawings of a large house, so I spoke to our local Vicar and got his permission to measure up and use the Vicarage for my submission.   It was quite a time consuming project and it took me several weeks to complete to my satisfaction, but it met the requirement OK.

 When we met, she told me that she had completed an apprenticeship in hairdressing and was working, with Bernard of Mayfair in Park Street, Bristol, by 1952 she was head girl there. In May I met Barbara's Grandad for the first time, a grand old man in his 90s, still earning good money doing hand tailoring. He reminded me of Ghandi, a very small man who sat cross legged in the centre of his huge cutting table with his work all around him. His mind was as sharp as a button and he was a very interesting man to listen to. He told a story of his school days, late 1800s, when one of the masters died and was laid out in the school hall. All the pupils were paraded past the coffin to pay their last respects, in one end of the hall and out of the other. He had just entered the hall when the master sat up in the coffin and pandemonium broke loose as everyone rushed for the doors. He was not dead, just in a coma! The doctors were not so good in those days and he was lucky that he came to before they put him in the ground! In June Barbara's brother married Rene and I was asked to be his best man. Barbara was fast becoming a key part of my life.

My back continued to give me a lot of trouble and I did very little racing and nothing of note in the cycling arena.

By July I had progressed well with the back exercises and reached the stage where it was not possible to hold any more books, so I bought a 120 lb set of barbells. I started on a general body building routine, with a half hour workout at home three times per week. The following year I joined Broad Plain Weightlifting Club, but it was to take me a few years before I could say that I had corrected the muscular imbalance. Also, I was unaware that it would eventually take me into the competitive world of Olympic Style weightlifting.

In March Phil Langford bought a new short wheelbase lightweight racing tandem and he and I started riding together, getting used to it, with a view to doing some tandem events. I rode front with Phil on the rear. We had no gears and rode a 90inch gear fixed wheel. Our first trip out we did Bristol/Weston Super Mare in 48mins and we were very happy with that. In May we did our first long ride, 170 mile day trip to south coast and back. June we broke the Club 30 mile tandem record with a time of 1- 05-25 and we started to look at the Mens Tandem records with a view to attacking a few of them. I had my eye on the Pembroke/London record, which I thought was well within our capabilities, but we needed to build our confidence with a series of longer distance races, so maybe the next year. Phil was happy to loan me the tandem from time to time, so in August Barbara

& I used it when feeding the riders at Fairford during the 12hr race and again in October when Barbara & I had our first trip away on our own for five days to Portsmouth, Bournemouth, Poole and home.

November saw me with my nose to the grindstone, with five days of examinations, covering ten subjects for the IAAS. And left me wondering if I had paid enough attention to my studies, so it was a great relief to get the results the following spring to find that I had passed the first exams.

Fighting back

1951 got off to a slow start, still suffering to a small degree from the back strain, but the regular training with the weights were having a significant effect, though not helping any with my racing form.

I was also courting seriously and looking back realise that I was perhaps a little less persistent with my training. However, on 27th May in pouring rain, I knocked 18minutes off of the Club Bristol/Taunton & back record and on 10th June I put up a reasonable performance winning the club Championship 50 mile with a 2.10.17. I was also pleased to find that despite my relatively poor season I would be receiving the Road Club Best All Rounder Award again.

I was beginning to feel it was time to push myself a bit workwise, having passed the first examination of the IAAS. September, I started work with Banks

Wood & Partners as a Worker Up, preparing Bills of Quantities and some final account work, with an increase in salary to £200 per annum! The office was only 200yds from the Salon where Barbara worked, so we were able to meet most days to have lunch together. I also received the first lessons of my correspondence course for the IAAS Intermediate examination and started to get back into the routine of studying again for a few evenings per week. Barbara & I made the most of the social season, attending a number of the Cycling Clubs Annual Dinners. At Xmas, Mum & Dad went to Pontypool as usual, while I spent four days with Barbara's family. While there, her brother Ron gave me my first driving lesson, though I had no cash and no expectation or desire to buy a car.

My racing in 1952 suffered somewhat from lack of hours in the saddle, the extra time with the weights building my body and trying to put extra hours in with my studies were no doubt the main reasons, but also serious courting probably had some effect

Late July, my friend Dave Dell & girlfriend Barbara, who later emigrated to Canada, joined Barbara & I on a canoe trip. We took our two homebuilt double Kayaks by train to Melksham and launched on the River Avon, camping on our way down river to Bristol. It was not the success that I had hoped for, as we had some showery days and some wet nights and Barbara did not seem keen to repeat the experience. I sold the Kayak shortly afterwards.

I now needed a 12hr result for the B,A.R competition, so I entered for the Yeovil 12hr. It was a very cold, miserable day, which seemed to get into my bones and I could find no speed in my legs. At 120 miles I decided that I had had enough and retired, the one and only time that I retired from a race for other than mechanical reasons. The one hour barrier for the 25mile out & home had recently been broken for the first time in the West of England and was a big talking point. One of our veteran members then put up a challenge, with the promise of a special award to any Club member of the Road Club who could break the hour in our Club Championship 25 on 26th September. I held the current Club 25 mile record with 1.0.27 and I decided that if that record had to go, then I must be the one to break it. A SW gale was blowing together with torrential rain. It was a hard flog into the wind out to the turn and a flyer coming back. I was passing cars parked at the side of the road, waiting for a respite in the weather as the wipers could not cope. Times were generally a lot slower than usual, however I won the event with a time of 1.0.37, only 10 seconds down on my best. I never did manage an under the hour 25, rare in those days, but a regular occurrence nowadays.

November 21st was a bad day for me, as I was given the sack by Banks Wood & Partners. However, it turned out to be a good lesson which served me well through life. One of the Senior Surveyors had left the firm and I was handed one of his Final Accounts, with the works 95% complete, to finish off at short notice.

I had to do the penultimate monthly payment and as I held the departing Surveyor in high esteem, I did not consider it necessary to check his workings to date. I was wrong, there were errors and it resulted in an overpayment to the Contractor. I was the scapegoat, but I vowed that no one would be allowed to drop me in it again. The following week I had five days of the IAAS Intermediate exams, ten subjects, to take my mind off of my joblessness. I need not have worried, I went around the corner to C.D.Radnedge, an IAAS office for interview, asking for a salary of £400 per annum. He offered me £350, but promised me £400 if I proved my worth in one month. I started 2nd December and found myself straight into a rush job, with plenty of overtime. Nothing further was said, but on my second pay day I found that I had a pay rise to £400 per annum. It was a small office with only five staff, other than the working boss, but a very happy little team to work with. Xmas came again and I stayed at Barbara's for four days. I think Mum & Dad were by this time sensing that things were getting serious between Barbara and I, as they came up for a visit one day to meet Bert and Laura.

My mileage for the year was a mere 8,000, well down on previous years, priorities obviously changing!

A year of change

1953 was a momentous year in my life, when everything seemed to be changing. Barbara and I were spending so much time together that our being in different cycling clubs was beginning to be a problem. However, I refused to join Bristol South and Barbara refused to join the Bristol Road Club, so we decided to join the Western Road Club, a fairly young Club with a very young membership. In fact there were so many courting couples in the Club that its nickname was "the Honeymoon Wheelers". I had also come to an impasse doing my weight training at home and I had joined Broad Plain Weightlifting Club. They had more weights and equipment available and I soon found myself involved with hand balancing and wrestling. In January I had the exam results and found that I had failed in three subjects, thereby failing totally. Had I failed in two subjects only I could have been referred to retake those subjects only. The deferment board wasted no time to inform me that my deferment from National Service was cancelled and I could expect call up at any time. Barbara and I talked about it and with the prospect of my being away for two years asked her to marry me. I remember mentioning the fact that I was a sportsman at heart and did not think that I would be likely to change. Luckily, she was also very sports minded and she agreed to marry me. We got engaged and celebrated it on Barbara's 21st birthday, Life then seemed to get rather hectic, arranging wedding date, invitations, bride and bridesmaid dresses to be made, photography etc. Bert and Laura offered us their back room and a bedroom to start our married life, so we started redecorating. I was still getting some racing in and on 1st March I was out on the road at 0600hrs to ride Bristol/Chippenham to arrive in time to start in the Chippenham 72 inch gear 25, but I did a mediocre ride due to lack of miles and no doubt had my mind on other things.

We were married at Filton Parish Church at 1400hrs on 4th April, my mother's birthday. Snow was falling as we came out of church, but we had only a 200yds walk to the reception at the Whitehouse Café, just across the road. We took the train to Torquay for our honeymoon, self-catering and ate out all week. We met another couple from the Club, Terry & Sheila, who were married the same day and were honeymooning at a hotel in Torquay. In fact twelve couples from the Western Road Club were also married that spring.

We decided to have a go and got down to a few weeks of training. May 23 to 25th, Barbara and I joined a crowd of newly marrieds from the Cycling Club for a camping weekend just outside Bristol. We dammed a stream to create a pool, practised balancing, variety of games, singing around the camp fire and down the local Pub in the evenings, altogether making a pretty memorable weekend. A few days later I attended for my Army Medical, classed A1 and was advised to expect call up pretty soon.

Saturday, May 30th, Tony & I rode tandem to Reading in company with Barbara and Tony's wife Joan on their solos. On the Sunday morning Tony & I competed in the Marlborough Tandem 50 at

Pangbourne Lane with a 93.6-inch fixed gear. We were on pretty good form, but it was a tough day with a hard slog into a strong wind to the turn. On the long drag up to the top of Speen Hill on the return, feeling the drag of our heavy tandem, we were passed by one of the fast pairs. That really put some fight into us and we were really winding it up going down the other side and must have been doing close to 50 mph as we entered Newbury. There was an old coaching house just past the first roundabout, with an archway and entrance under the building to a central yard. Just as we arrived a heavy cart horse, pulling a heavy wagon emerged from this archway, blocking half the width of the road. My thoughts were that our chances of clearing the horse were 50/50, but I shouted to Tony to duck his head as I steered under the horse's head. The horse reared and whinnied and we were through. We did not dare to look back and thanked our lucky stars that it was early on a Sunday morning and there were no police about. We were very pleased with our time 1hr 57min only 7mins behind the winners.

National Service
6th August 1953 was the day when my life took a drastic change. I reported at Norton Camp, Worcester for two years compulsory National Service in the Royal Engineers I was billeted in a Nissen hut with a tough crowd of Geordies, mainly steel erectors.. The following day we had our interviews for

job allocation. I had asked for Quantity Surveying Assistant and was accepted as such. The camp itself was very rough, very lacking in comfort and the food was atrocious. Coming straight from good home cooking it was hard to take and at every meal many of the chaps would push their plates back hardly touched. In those days, with all my cycling and weight training I had a very big appetite and I was regularly clearing other people's plates. It was a whole new world, marching, drill training and foul mouthed, bigoted little lance corporals acting like little Gods. Luckily, I was very fit and did not find it physically exacting, it was the discipline that irked me. On the Sunday we did have a day of rest and the Geordies were out on the grass doing some wrestling. I joined in and having done a bit in the Gym, I was able to give a fair account of myself. Then along came one of the obnoxious Lance Corporals. He was in uniform and carrying a rifle. He watched us for short while, then said "So you fancy yourselves at wrestling eh, well let's see you stop this" and as he stepped forward he started to swing his rifle at us, while holding the barrel. The Geordie that I was wrestling with stepped quickly to the side and before he could blink, the corporal went flying in one direction and his rifle in another. We never got bothered again. We were not at that camp for long thank goodness and I was never again exposed to such rough living. I was convinced that it was intended to break moral before getting us involved in the serious training. Before leaving, I was elected as spokesman for our hut and had to meet the Commanding Officer to tell him what we had thought of our initiation at the camp. I spared nothing and told him exactly what a lousy camp he ran, particularly in respect of the food. He took it all without any comment.

I was then moved to the training camp at Malvern. What a contrast, the food was great, with usually a choice and plenty of it. The camp was clean and gave you a feeling of efficiency, but the training was intense and very little time for yourself. Within a week I was offered a WOSB, officer training. However I was told that it would not be in the Quantity Surveying field and after consideration I thought two years away from Surveying would put me back to square one on return to Civvy Street, so I said "No thanks". They had a very good Gym at the camp and I used to spend any spare time that I had working out. If there were any extra jobs to be done, the NCO's would grab anyone who happened to be lying on their bunks, so it gave me great satisfaction in avoiding that. I was just a quarter inch short of 6 feet, which was pretty tall in those days, so on field training days I always seemed to be picked to carry the Bren Gun in addition to my own kit. However, when it came to the forced marches, march a quarter mile, then run a quarter with full kit, I felt sorry for the small guys. There was one very game little Welshman, around 8 stone, who was always struggling on the runs, so we got him between me and another big chap. When he was lagging we would each hook a finger under his belt and his feet hardly touched the ground. We had our Pass Out Parade on 8th December and Barbara came up with her mother, my mother and my sister. After the Parade we all went into Malvern for a meal before seeing them on the train. The following day I travelled to Royal Engineers School of Military Engineering, Chatham.

Brompton Barracks was an old type Barracks, very drafty and not a lot of heating. Washing facilities were truly archaic, consisting of an open ended building with stone floors and no hot water or heating! no home comforts here. For the next eleven weeks I was learning the Military Services ways of dealing with building works, including the War Department Forms of Contract and the War Department Schedule of Rates, which we would be used for pricing works. I was taken aside by one of the chaps who had been there a while and told that it was only necessary for me to go on morning parade every third day. This seemed very odd to me, but he explained, that there were a number of courses running concurrently, including Clerks of Works, Plant operator, etc. and there were continually people being posted in and posted out. The Sergeant Major did not have a clue how many should be there and it was best to keep him guessing. This was my first introduction to Bullshit baffles brains, very useful in the army! There was a Nissen hut set up for weightlifting and I was down there two or three evenings per week. Wednesday afternoons were sports afternoon and I always used it for a cycle run, having taken my bike up at first opportunity. Then one day a notice went up, listing the teams for the 5 mile cross country race to be held the following Wednesday and my name was on it. I went into the camp office and told them that they had made a mistake, I was a cyclist, not a runner. They said it was no mistake as all cycling had been cancelled that week. I had never run more than one mile and that had been at Grammar School, some seven years earlier, so I thought OK I will just take it easy. However, I was very fit and on the day at the two mile point I found that I was catching a few. I came to a five-bar gate and a runner was laboriously climbing over it. Without thinking I put one hand on the top bar and vaulted it as I usually did with gates. However, I was making no allowance for the two miles just run, my foot caught the top bar and I finished up face down in the mud on the other side. I think I must have got angry at this point, cursing the stupid Army bods who put me in for this. My competitive spirit came to the fore, I pressed on harder and I surprised myself by finishing twelfth. Next day was a different story, when I tried to get out of the bed. I found my muscles seized up and had to roll out of bed.

I was making the effort to get home every weekend, but my pay was peanuts and did not even cover my fare to Bristol & Back, so Barbara was having to subsidise the cost of my return trip. I then heard that one of the Sergeants travelled home to Bristol every weekend on his motorcycle, so I pall'd up with him and travelled with him for the price of a one-way fare, but wow, did I suffer with some very cold rides in late autumn. My course ended mid-November and was automatically promoted to Lance Corporal Quantity Surveying Assistant and was then awaiting posting. In the meantime, I had to report every morning for general duties. I was immediately allocated to the tarmac squad, preparing for and laying tarmac paths. It proved to be hard graft and lasted three days. The day we finished the job we were told that was it for the day and I went back to my room, feeling completely knackered and flopped on my bunk. The Sergeant came around and seeing me on my bunk started shouting and accusing me of skiving. Well I leapt off the bunk and gave him a piece of my mind. He walked out without a further word, but next morning at job allocation, I was given a job at the post Office, one of the best jobs available and I stayed on that for the rest of my time there. I was then informed that I had been posted to Egypt and I was given leave for a few days. I went to Bristol and brought Barbara back to Chatham for a change. We stayed at the NAAFI Club, very comfortable, explored Chatham & Gillingham, had a day in London, Petticoat Lane, London Bridge, Tower of London etc. and dancing at the Club in the evenings. Sunday 6th December, I put her on the train at Paddington and next day I signed out of SME. I then moved down the road to Transit and found that the accommodation there was even rougher than. Brompton Barracks. I was there for one week and every day we all paraded for work allocation. There were two of us who used the Gym regularly and the Sergeant was also a lifter, so every day we tucked our training gear under our arms as we went on parade. The sergeant questioned what we were carrying, so we said it was in case there was no work we were ready to go training. It paid off as every day he seemed to run out of jobs before he got to us.

A Trip Overseas

It came as a bit of a shock to find myself posted overseas and on15th December our detachment entrained to London and then on to Googe Street Underground for flight to Egypt. This was an old disused tube station which had been taken over as accommodation for servicemen in transit. There were five QSA's in my draft and we were due to move pm the following day, so we were free to go out on the town for the evening. I arrived back at Googe Street around midnight to find a message awaiting, telling me to report to the office immediately on my return. I wandered up to the office, which was open 24hrs daily, wondering what I could possibly have done wrong! It appeared that someone from the previous draft had gone sick and my name had been picked out as the lucky guy to replace him. Unfortunately, it meant that I had to be up at 0400 in time to catch the transport, I felt anything but lucky at that moment. We were at Stanstead Airport for 07.30 take-off, only to find it fog bound and we were eventually on our way at 10.15. It was my first ever flight and it was a long one by today's standards. We stopped for two hours at Malta for refuelling and arrived at Fayal, Egypt at 01.30hrs where I was accommodated in a tent. The following morning, I found myself ushered in to see the Chief Engineer Middle East for interview. It was then that I realised how lucky I had been. He said that he had five positions to fill, one in Cyprus and four in various parts of Egypt and as I was the first of the QSA's to arrive I could take my pick. I had done my homework and knew that Egypt was a rough posting, with many problems and virtually no chance of getting Barbara out to join me, so I chose Cyprus. That afternoon Steve whom I had palled up with at Chatham, heard that I had arrived and looked me up. He was working in the office, he knew the ways of the camp and put me wise as to how to avoid unnecessary hassle. He told me to leave my tent at a certain time every morning and walk slowly clockwise around the camp in order to avoid the regular tent inspections. If they don't get used to seeing your face they will never know you have arrived. As he worked in the office, he was able to get a pass to take him through the gate every day and spend the afternoon at the Yacht Club down on the Bitter Lake. So we used to add my name under his and we enjoyed our afternoons. One day we stayed a little late and it was getting dark as we left the Club. As we walked up the road we saw three Arabs in dirty robes approaching and looking pretty menacing. Steve said "Watch these, one hand on your money and be ready to hit them hard and run". I thought Hells Bells I didn't bargain for this. We need not have worried as just then an army five tonner came up the road. The driver obviously assessed the situation, pulled alongside and shouted "Get Aboard" We both dived over the tailboard and sighed with relief. There had been a few cases of soldiers being knifed around that time. I spent one week at the camp in Fayal and it stands out in my mind as one of the worst weeks of my life. I had never been mollycoddled and I was used to camping and a bit of roughing it, but there was nothing in that camp that I could say a good word about. It was smelly, dirty, the food was lousy and I was lucky that I had a friend there who knew the ropes and helped me make the best of it.

23rd December I was on the plane on my way to Cyprus where I moved into the Corporals Mess, Nicosia, a collection of Nissen huts, but I was suitably impressed. No parades, no bullshit, waiter service and great food and I was in time for the Xmas festivities. Xmas Eve I was awakened at 0800hrs with Gunfire (tea laced with rum) in my bunk served by the Sergeants. Breakfast was at 1000hrs and later in the day we had a sumptuous dinner served by the officers. . I thought that I must be dreaming, could this be the same army! I was happy that things seemed to be on the way up all of a sudden, but I was missing Barbara. In those days telephoning international could only be done by visiting the Cable Co and booking a call at quite a cost and I was not aware of the procedure, so I spent a lot of time writing long letters home. It was the 28th December when I met the Chief Engineer Cyprus, who would decide my fate. He decided to keep me at the chief Engineers Office at Nicosia, which meant that I had finally arrived and no more moves. Saturday 2nd

January, I went to a party at Mr Walkers, Warrant Officer Quantity Surveyor at CRE and had a wonderful evening, with good company and plenty of good food. Little was I to know at that time that before leaving Cyprus, I would be taking over his job as a Staff Sargent.

One of the first things on arrival in Nicosia was to make enquiries as to the possibilities of getting Barbara out to join me. However, I soon came to the conclusion that it would be a very poor existence on National Service Pay with the minimal allowances that I would be entitled to. I talked to Gordon Scott, the Pay Sergeant, who advised me that if I signed on for three years' service, Barbara could be out within three months and we would be able to manage nicely on the allowances. I wrote to Barbara, told her the facts and she immediately replied "sign on". I had a medical on the 5th January 1954, passed A1 and signed on for three years on 7th January, with four years on the reserve and immediately applied for a passage out for Barbara. . I had never been very impressed with the heavy Khaki uniform that I had been issued with, so I took it to the Garrison Taylor and had it tailored to fit me properly, making a vast difference and I was far happier. Corporal John Rushdon, a cross country runner approached me, trying to persuade me to run in the forthcoming 6 mile Army Cross Country Race. I told him that I was not a runner, but as I was without a bike, why not. As a result, I was out running most days with him and John Pollard. On the 8th January the three of us ran to the start of cross-country course, ran around the course and then ran back to the lines, eleven miles in total and felt pretty confident about our chances. The race was on the 10th and we wiped the floor with the prizes. John Rushdon was first, John Pollard second and myself third. John Pollard also picked up first handicap prize and I got the second. I missed my bike, so I applied for an Army issue bike, an off the shelf sports bike. It was a far cry from my own hand-built bike, but would make me mobile till my own arrived. We worked only mornings, so with the afternoons free I was able to explore the island. My first trip took me over the 1,300 ft, Mountain Pass, involving several hairpins, to Kyrenia on the beautiful north coast, around trip of 34 miles. Mid-January I rode to Larnaca on the south coast and got talking to a Scotsman, who told me that he had been a racing cyclist. He invited me back to his place for lunch, where I met his wife Cynthia and his family. He was also a QS, but a civilian working at the Larnaca office and unknown to me at that time, we were destined to cross paths again many years later, when he would be working for me. In addition to the cycling I was also out running 3 to 4 evenings per week, which varied from 5 to 12 miles, so was in pretty good shape and enjoying army life much better than I had expected.

The education Officer insisted that I take the 2nd class education exam. I argued that the RICS entry exam which I had passed, exempted me from these tests. He would not be persuaded so, cussed as I am, I wrote direct to the Army Chief Education Officer. A week later I was advised that he had confirmed that I was not required to take the 2nd or 1st army tests. In the office I was involved with a variety of jobs, nothing very exciting and quite a step down from what I had been used to. One day the Deputy office boss came to me with a lengthy, double foolscap schedule containing many columns of figures. In those days we had no copying machines and he wanted an exact copy. He wanted it accurate, he wanted it neat and he was in a hurry! I got busy and an hour later he was back to see if I had finished, but I was a long way from finished! A half hour later he was back again, I was only a lowly Lance Corporal, but I slowly turned to face him and said "You want it accurate, you want it neat and you want it fast, I'm afraid you can't have all three". He did'nt say a word, he disappeared and when I took it to him about an hour later, he thanked me and we got on well after that

I had by now got involved with the RAF Cycling group and did a few runs with them. Mid -March three of us set off for Troodos, 6,400 ft, which would be the longest climb that I had ever done. At Kekapatria, 2,400 ft, the RAF boys turned back and I went on to the top alone, arriving there around 1300hrs, where I met up with a crowd from the office. The snow was deep and I was in shorts and short sleeved shirt, but the sun was out and I enjoyed tobogganing with them for an hour or so before heading back. It was a thrilling run down the mountain with the many steep hairpins to negotiate. I was back in time for dinner, having clocked up a tough 102 miles.   Another new interest to pass the time was horse riding. There was a Cypriot living near the barracks who had a few horses for hire and a few of us used to enjoy a bit of a gallop through the woods. A bit different from my riding in Wales, we actually had saddles and proper reins. All good fun

Barbara was expected 19th March. Three days before she arrived, I was struck with horrendous tooth ache and I had virtually no sleep for two nights. I was not happy to go to the Army dentist, so on the 18th I visited a private dentist that I had met at the Yacht Club. He said that I had an abscess under the tooth and it would have to come out. I told him that my wife was due next day, so he gave me a double injection and told me to hang on tight to the chair. I thought that he was pulling my head off, but he got it out in one piece and showed me the tooth with the abscess hanging underneath, what a relief! He told me to come back that same afternoon when he would fit another tooth to my plate, so that I would look respectable when my wife arrived. I was very impressed with him and he became a very good friend of mine.

Barbara arrived on time on and she was a little bewildered at how different things were compared to England. The first time that I took her into the town, a vehicle came along, no glass in the windows and with goats and chickens at the rear. She could not believe me when I said "Here we are, this is the bus".

That weekend we went off with friends in their car. Barbara took to Connie right away, they became our closest friends during our Cyprus days and in fact, friends for life. I had taken 14 days leave and enjoyed showing Barbara around Nicosia, introducing her to open air Cinemas and how to bargain in the shop. The message soon spread that she was a good hairdresser and it wasn't long before she found herself regularly doing friends hair at home.

Early April I bought a 90cc Tiger Cub Motor cycle, which proved to be a problem from word go and seemed to spend nearly as much time back with the agent as on the road. In August I returned it for the seventh time and insisted on my money back. I then ordered an AJS 500cc single cylinder bike, which I collected late August. In the meantime, I had passed the Army Motor Cycle test and was able to drop the L plates and carry Barbara. Our working day during the summer was from 0730hrs to 1300hrs, Monday to Saturday, so I had plenty of time to get involved in every aspect of sport that was going. The army did encourage it and there was no problem with time off if representing the unit. I was in the Tug of War team and Putting the shot in the Cyprus Army sports day. I was in the swimming team for the Army v RAF Gala in August and then joined the Royal Engineers Nicosia Water Polo team. I was never a keen player in ball games, as I never seemed to have any idea where the ball would be going, but Water Polo seemed different and I revelled in it. In fact, we proved to be a pretty good team, beating the RAF, the local Police and all other challengers. However, when the Para troop Regt arrived, we took our first thrashing. I remember my shock when I saw their team at the pool, their smallest chap was as big as our biggest and did they play rough. They sure knew how to use their feet and I seem to remember spending half the game under water. Late August I was also in the unit team for the Army Swimming Gala, swimming the 200yds freestyle and the 600yd relay. Now that we had reliable transport our weekends and spare afternoons were usually spent at the Services Yacht Club at Kyrenia, on the north coast, sailing Snipes and on Sundays crewing in a Wildcat for the Major. In September I got my dinghy ticket and started helming myself in the races with Barbara as my crew. We finished the sailing season with all the boats taking a moonlight sail to Snake Island, 1.5miles westward, for a late-night picnic. We were certainly enjoying the varied and active lifestyle of Nicosia and a very different type of Army life from that which I had known in UK. Barbara and I were also enjoying the nightlife of Nicosia at the various Night Clubs,

All was not in fact totally rosy as there were a few riots by the ENOSIS group, wanting union with Greece. These were easily quelled at first and had little effect on our way of life, but we did not at that time appreciate just what they would lead to. However, it did have the effect of making me realise that I was in fact in the Army and not just working in another office. The next big event in the offing was the Army Cycling Championship Cyprus, a massed start race of 47miles to be run over a course on the south of the island late October. Luckily by this time my own bike had arrived from England and I wanted to enter a team from our unit. There were two other cyclists who were interested, but they did not have their own bikes. With a bit of pushing we managed to acquire two bikes from Army Sports, not exactly what we would have chosen, but all working and complete with three gears. We gave them a good going over and they got into training. 17th October I did my own final training run, 110 miles to Troodos & back, riding every one of the 6,700ft to the summit. On the day, 23 October, the weather was good, but quite a strong norwest wind, a following wind for the last 12 miles of the race. I had never taken part in a massed start race, so was not well versed in team tactics. However, at the 12miles point Ray was still with me in the leading bunch of six, when his rear spindle stripped, so he dropped out and I found myself on my own. I had no trouble staying with the group, but wondered what my chances were of making a break. My chance came at 29mile, when on a short climb, there was a breakaway by two riders and a chase for a quarter mile to bring them back in the bunch. As soon as they were all settled I broke clean away and none had the energy to catch me. I increased my lead to six minutes and won in the time of 2.22.55. I was interviewed by the British Forces Broadcasting and amazed at the fuss over a 47mile race as I listened to the broadcast the following day.

Late October Barbara & I were invited to Mr Hurd's (Chief Quantity Surveyor) party. We had a wonderful evening, but when we left at around midnight, we found our new motor cycle had been stolen. It was found abandoned by the Police the following day, minus the Headlamp and battery and it was about one month before the agent could provide us with replacements. Shortly after that my set of weights arrived from England and I could resume training in my garage, often joined by my friend Vic. Also Andreas and Vassos, the two Greek lads from next door, often joined me, despite all the growing anti-British feelings amongst the Greeks.

I had applied for a correspondence course to study for the RICS first examination and it was about this time that the local Education Officer, Major Durante, turned down my application on the grounds that the regulations limited courses to four subjects and my course consisted of 10 subjects. I argued my case with the Major on the grounds that the RICS would not allow me to take the exam four subjects at a time, but to no avail. I then wrote direct to the Chief Education Officer of the British Army and within a month I had the course that I wanted, proving that, even in the Army, there are exceptions to every rule if you have a good case. Mid December 1954 there was trouble threatening again and I was on guard duty two nights with the rest of the Unit, protecting vital installations. There was a growing awareness that the trouble was escalating and not likely to go away, but so far had little effect on our very pleasant way of life. It was Barbara's first Xmas away from her family, but we had a very good one with good friends and plenty going on. I had a further bit of good fortune when I received another promotion to substantive Sergeant.

The Troodos Mountains with its beautiful snowy cap was beckoning to us early in 1955, so 5th February we rode to the Services Ski Camp for a week's skiing. We rode up on the AJS, arriving in a snow storm, very tricky on two wheels. I don't know if they took pity on half frozen Barbara, but we were allocated an Officers log cabin with the log fire already lit and were soon very cosy. The following day the thaw set in, but there was still a lot of snow at Mount Olympus, 6miles further up. We did a great deal of walking, down to the Seven Sisters and to Caledonian Falls. Then on the Wednesday we hired the necessary equipment, got a lift to the top and enjoyed our first ever days skiing. It was just as well as the rest of the week we had heavy rain and skiing was out.

By this time Barbara was working regular at Michael's hair salon in Nicosia and I was training with the Motor Cycle Trials team every week. I was trying to talk Barbara into a motor cycle tour on the Continent, for our Summer Break, but she was set on going back to England to see her folk, she was homesick! I then came up with the bright idea of combining the two, a motor cycle trip across Europe to UK & back, 6,000 miles plus in six weeks? She did not think it viable, so I set about planning just that. I didn't have much of a clue what it involved, but I bought maps, then wrote to the AA for advice. They came up trumps with proposed route and places of interest on the way and the whole idea grew from there. I fitted rear carrier and twin panniers on the AJS and Keith loaned us a tent. The next job was to research the means of getting to Athens and booked a passage on the ferry to Athens for 10th August, returning 17th September. I then went ahead and booked my whole years 6 weeks leave to start 10th August, crossing my fingers that nothing would crop up to put a spanner in the works.

It was known that the terrorists were hiding out in the Troodos mountains and a British Army unit was deployed to flush them out. Unfortunately, the terrorists knew the terrain better than our troops, led them into a trap, then started a forest fire. A lot of soldiers were caught in the fire and perished. This coincided with a suspicious accident to the staff bus carrying several of our senior ranks on the daily run from Larnaca. The bus collided with another heavy vehicle, the driver of which leapt from the cab just before impact and disappeared? The funerals for the unfortunates who died was combined with that for forest fire victims and was quite a major event. I was one of the bearers for one of our Warrant Officers and the procession involved several vehicles en route to the cemetery. I will never forget the way the villagers disappeared and slammed their front doors as we drove through the village.

The tension seemed to be building fast!An additional problem in mid-May, when I hit a suicidal dog and we came off the motor bike. I hurt my knee and wrist and Barbara was badly shaken up. One week later, with an even more painful wrist I drove to the hospital for check, where an X ray showed that I had broken a bone in the wrist. It was reset and stayed in plaster for six weeks. It was quite a handicap, putting a stop to my weight training, time trialling with the RAF boys and a number of other activities. However, I could ride the motor bike OK and it did not stop me swimming, as I soon found it easy enough to swim with one arm, with the other held high out of the water. There were some serious problems with EOKA terrorists in July, security was really tightened up and rumours were circulating that all leave could be cancelled.

I was seriously worried that all my plans for the trip to UK could be scuppered, in addition to all the expenditure which could be wasted. However, Barbara was in the habit of going to the Colonels house to cut and set his wife's hair and I always dropped her there to pick her up. Quite often when I was waiting for her the Colonel would join me for a chat, so I took the opportunity to put the question to him. He could see my dilemma and told me not to worry, my leave would not be cancelled. He did not give me that in writing, but I did feel reassured and carried on with my plans.

Fate was still having a go, as I came across an oil spillage on the road mid-July, I came off the bike again with Barbara on the back, only a few hundred yards from the previous crash and broke a bone in the other wrist. Another trip to hospital to get plastered up and they told me to come back in six weeks for it to be removed. I told them that I was supposed to be on my way to UK by motorcycle in five weeks' time, so could I have it off a week early. They were not very happy, but agreed and suggested that an elasticated wrist strap would be advisable for the first few days driving. By now I was beginning to wonder if there was anything else that could happen before we left.

A trip of a life time

On 10th August we drove to Limassol, boarded the steamer and enjoyed a very relaxing passage to Athens. As there was no Yugoslav Embassy in Cyprus, we had to get our Visa in Athens, so while waiting we had time to visit the Acropolis, before setting up camp down on the coast. We collected our Visa on the 13th before heading for the border, 400 miles north, but were satisfied with an easy 140 miles on our first day. The roads were pretty rough and we camped just short of the border, crossing at 0730 am on the 15th. My passport had me down as British Army and I had a nasty reception by the Greek Border Guards, who actually spat at my feet and stretched my control to the limit. However, I kept my cool and we were eventually through to Yugoslavia, as it was called then, a communist country firmly under the control of Tito. Our lunch time stop that day was in a respectable hotel. The restaurant was pretty busy with a lot of chatter going as we started to eat. Then suddenly all chatter ceased and we looked up to see that two armed police had walked in, with hands on the butts of their revolvers as they had a thorough look around. They said nothing, but they opened every door and checked it out before leaving. It took a few moments after their departure before conversation resumed and we were left in no doubt that we were in a police state. Our first night in Yugoslavia we had torrential rain and we found to our horror that the borrowed tent leaked abominably. At first light we were up, packing and on the road by 07.30 am. The dirt roads were in a terrible state, plenty of mud and we even found a bridge washed away. Luckily the flood had subsided when we reached it and I was grateful for my trials training as I picked my way across the river bed, weaving my way between the boulders and managing to avoid deep water. I was glad that we were on a motorcycle as it would not have been possible for a car. We could not speak the language and at meal times we depended on being able to point out the food that we wanted, but it was always good basic food, plenty of it and not expensive. I always sampled their beer at lunchtime and their wine at night and we always fared very well. However, when Barbara decided that she wanted a milk shake I found that a little problem. I resorted to mime, milking a cow, pouring it into a container, shaking it thoroughly, then drinking it and wonder of wonders, Barbara got her milkshake in addition to a few hysterics!

We were taking a lot of photos and in one village, with a dirt road, a raised wooden walkway and a beautiful church spire at the end of the street, I just stopped and pulled out the camera. Within minutes there was pandemonium, a policeman rushed over and shouted "No photografe" as he tried to grab my camera. I immediately sat on it and shouted back. Another uniformed man arrived demanding the camera, but I continued to argue that he should be proud of his beautiful village and happy to have it photographed. A crowd had by now gathered around us, but no one saying a word apart from the officials. The arguing went on for some time, then the uniformed man seemed to relent and said "OK, but no photographs between here and Belgrade. We got to the end of the street and realized what all the fuss was about, next to the church was a huge barracks. Despite the conditions we managed 240miles that day, reaching Belgrade, the capital, by 7.00 pm, where we booked into a hotel for the night. Our sleeping bags were wet so we draped them on the hot water pipes and managed to dry them out somewhat! We had a late start next day, but we were then on an Autostrada and had a fast run to Zagreb, where we found ourselves back on dirt roads. With 296 miles under our belt we called at a farmhouse, where we were allowed to sleep in their barn. Off again at 7.30 am, but the rough roads were taking their toll and at 20miles we had our first puncture. Midday we reached Postojna Grottoes, a huge cave network. We were taken one kilometre underground by narrow gauge rail and had a conducted tour of some fantastic caverns, some with lakes inhabited by blind lizards and certainly worth the minor detour to visit it. Mid afternoon we carried on, crossing the border into Italy and had afternoon tea in Trieste, which seemed so civilised after the wilds of Yugoslavia. We carried on in the dark for some miles and found ourselves a comfortable B & B for the night. We were now enjoying some pleasant riding on good roads and Friday 19th August saw us heading for Venice. We spent all our cash on a trip in a Gondola and had to visit the bank to get more cash for lunch, but it was definitely a highlight in our trip. We carried on north to Milan and spent the night at a campsite in the centre of the city. It was a well organised site, with a series of enclosures between 5 feet hedges. Before leaving Milan next day we paid a visit to Milan Cathedral, a truly majestic building with many spires. We drove around Lake Como and on past Lake Lugano before heading into Switzerland. The scenery was fantastic as we headed up into the Alps, but we also wondered if we had brought enough clothes with us as we progressed higher. We went over the St Gothard and then the Furka Pass, where we saw the Rhone Glacier and entered a grotto within the ice. However, by the end of the day we were over the high Alps and found a lovely Swiss campsite in the valley. Next day we crossed into France, over the Jura Mountains and camped at a large registered camp at Dijon just as it was getting dark. Monday, 22nd was our last day in France as we headed into Paris, where we had time to visit Notre Dame and climb the Eiffel Tower. That evening we camped just outside Cherbourg and caught the early morning flight, motor cycle and all, over to Southampton.

Our arrival in UK, 23rd August 1955, coincided with a heat wave and we were surprised to be riding in shirt sleeves. That evening we got our tandem out and rode to the Western Road Club meeting to meet our cycling friends. 25th August we set off on the AJS for Brighton. The heat wave was still holding and we were happy in shirt sleeves all the way.

Many of our cycling friends, Architect, Surveyor, Plumber, Bricklayer, Electrician etc. ten couples in all, had banded together to form a self-help housing group and over the next 5 to 6 years succeeded in moving into their own self build homes, a fantastic achievement. two weeks at home flew by and Monday 5th September was spent saying many farewells, ready for an early start on the 6th

We were on the road by 07.30 next day, to Southampton to catch the 1100 flight. We were in Paris by mid-morning on the 7th, where we had to collect our Visas for Yugoslavia and were not back on the road again until 16.30. After a wet night we headed over the Alps, through Mont Cenis Pass into Italy and had a very wet ride through Turin and on to a big camp site at Genoa. We were pleased to find that we could rent a large tent, already erected, and we would not have to erect our own small tent in the torrential rain. There was also a good restaurant on the site, so our wet and miserable day did not end too badly. Another wet and miserable day on the 9th, through La Spezia to Pisa, where we climbed to the top of the leaning tower, then on to Florence and over the mountains in the dark to Bologna, where we pitched camp around midnight. We then headed east across the lowlands of Italy and over the border into Yugoslavia. All seemed to be going well until the rear brake cable failed and I knew that I must get it fixed before crossing the next range of mountains. We stopped in the centre of Mostar and a curious crowd soon formed around us. I had a problem, how was I to communicate with these people when I could not speak a word of their language. I stripped off the broken cable and looked around for an intelligent face. I walked over to him, smiled and held up the cable and showed him the nipple which should have been attached to the end. He smiled back and beckoned for me to follow him, so I called across to Barbara to stay with the bike while I was gone. I was taken to a building site, where someone produced some solder and soldering iron, then lit a fire in the garden. It was as basic as one could get, but I managed to secure the nipple to the cable without an intelligible word exchanged and there were big smiles all round as I shook his hand and patted him on the back. I returned to the bike to find Barbara hard pressed by onlookers and trying hard to keep her composure, as she was being well and truly bitten by midges. However, we were soon on our way again and the cable did not fail.

Our second day in Yugoslavia, the clouds started to pile up and heavy rain threatening, so we decided to eat early and hopefully get the tent pitched before the rain came. We drove into a picturesque little village and were aware of the smell of cooked food. We followed our noses to a rough old shack and it smelt truly appetizing. We went in to find a single room with several basic wood tables, a dirt floor and a big wood fired range in the corner with several pots set in the top. There was a buxom woman by the range who lifted the covers of the various pots to show what was available. The food looked and smelled good, so we made our choice and found a table. The old Dear brought our food over, together with some cutlery and we tucked in with a vengeance. Barbara gave me a nudge and pointed out that we seemed to be the only ones with cutlery and that the old fellow at the next table didn't seem to have taken his eyes off us. I finished my food and decided that another helping would go down well, I did have a good appetite in those days! I got up and wandered over to the old Dear with my plate and as I did so, the old boy at the next table jumped up, grabbed Barbara's knife and fork, went back to his own table and carried on eating his own food using her cutlery. The old Dear saw this, she quickly rushed over, cuffed him round the ears, took the knife and fork, wiped them in her dirty apron and gave them back to Barbara. Barbara was nonplussed and immediately lost her appetite, so we made our departure and did manage to find a suitable site on which to pitch the tent before the rains came.

The rains had turned the dirt roads to mud and I was glad of my training with the trials team, but the next incident was really a surprise and a painful one. I was driving through a fairly wooded stretch, doing a steady 40 to 45 mph, along a fairly muddy section, when I suddenly felt pressure, followed by a searing pain across my mouth and we came off the bike. Someone had stretched a string across the road, at head height, in the way that they did during the war using wire. It was lucky for me that it was only string, which broke and cut both sides of my mouth. It left me with a bloody and painful mouth and for three days I was trying to talk with minimum movement of my lips.

We were on a pretty tight programme for reaching Athens in time for our ship home, so with poor weather added to the other problems encountered, we were very concerned when the bike started to lose power. It was losing oil, overheating and top speed dropped to 40mph.

We carried on for a few days, making up for lack of speed by travelling a few hours longer each day. Then with only three days to go before catching the boat, the bike stopped early morning and just refused to start again. We were way out in the sticks, I had only basic tools with me, we had had no breakfast and we had only soup and drinks to keep us going until we could make it to the town. I had visions of missing the boat and being "Absent without leave", a serious offence in the army! I would not in any way describe myself as a competent mechanic, however, in desperation I set about doing a top overhaul at the roadside. It was late afternoon by the time I had it all back together, by which time I had achieved somewhat better compression and oil seemed to be reaching the necessary parts, but the spark was too weak. I had carried a spare spark plug all the way, until we came across a Yugoslav stranded north of Belgrade a few days earlier. Thinking we were nearing the end of our journey; I had given him my one and only plug to get him on his way. Now there was no kind soul at hand to do the same for me. It was getting dusk and there was nothing to do other than head for the nearest town, two miles back in the direction that we had come. I could not leave Barbara with the bike out in the wilds, while I walked to the town and back, so I pushed the bike, all of 450lbs plus a full load of luggage. I was very glad that I was in good shape, but I was glad of an extra push from Barbara on the hills. We made it to the town, we found what we considered to be the nearest thing to a garage, but it was closed. We eventually found the owner and then had a further shock when he told us the price of a spark plug. There were few motorised vehicles in Yugoslavia at that time and they must have been considered an expensive luxury. Even the Army used horse drawn vehicles as their main means of transport. We then appreciated why the fellows had been so profuse with their thanks at the free gift of a plug a few days earlier. We were getting low on Yugoslav Dinars, we were not sure how far to the nearest Bank, we hadn't had a proper meal since the previous day and if I paid the price being asked, we could possibly be on the ship before we had our next one. Luckily, he had a friend who spoke French and I was able to relate our problem. I told him that if he let me have the plug, I would send him two from Cyprus. After such a day I must have been looking pretty haggard, or maybe I had an honest face, but whatever the reason he gave me the plug and we were on our way again. I did send him the plugs as promised with a thank you note in French, but I never knew whether he received it OK, or if he had any problems with customs. The bike was performing, but sluggish and I was far from happy. We drove late that night in order to give ourselves a safe chance of reaching Athens the following day, the day before our departure. We pitched our tent late on the 16th September, on the outskirts of Athens and it was with great relief when we boarded the ship the following morning. We then enjoyed a relaxing few days aboard, arriving Cyprus on the 19th, to surprise my Warrant Officer. I am sure, judging by certain comments, that he was annoyed at my rapid, substantive promotion. He had expressed opinions that I was crazy to embark on such a trip and was, I am sure, disappointed that he could not charge me with being absent without leave. It had been one hell of an adventure, but I never let him know just how close it had been.

Troubled times ahead

In the short time that we had been away the troubles had escalated, there were shootings from time to time and we were issued with arms. As another rank I was issued with a sten gun, which I thought rather stupid as I had never fired a sten gun and furthermore no one bothered to ask if I was familiar with the weapon. Night patrols were then organised in every district on a roster. We would patrol to an irregular pattern, two soldiers each night and I found myself on this duty usually once per week. From then on, we were to find ourselves subject to tighter security, which tended to strangle the social life that we had previously enjoyed. Daytime activities were not so much affected and we were able to carry on sailing, but if we went inside the city wall, Barbara got in the habit of walking a hundred yards behind me, so that she could shout a warning if anyone pointed a gun at my back. I had never liked using the Army barber, as he was too inclined to cut it his way, short back and sides. However, I changed my mind when front page of the local paper showed a grizzly picture of a Cypriot, reputedly an informer, sitting in the barber's chair at the establishment that I usually used, with his throat cut.

In October 1955, an advertisement of an MG TC model caught my eye and with my increase in pay, I thought "Why not". I had had a few driving lessons on an army one tonner, with a crash gearbox, but I had no licence. However, I bought the MG, drove it home and put it in my garage and put my AJS up for sale. I drove the MG around for a few weeks, but keeping well outside the city walls, then applied for a local test. The day of the test came and I had to pick up the examiner at his home. He had me drive around some of the back streets of Nicosia, then told me to stop at a certain house. It appeared that it was the house of his Landlord and he needed to pay his rent. The test lasted twenty minutes, without incident and I was told that I had passed.

In April 56 the troubles came a little too close to home when I came face to face with a terrorist for the first time. On my way to the office, 200yds from my house I saw two youths pointing pistols and shooting at a Greek neighbour who worked for the Brits. I stopped my car, grabbed my sten gun, but the strap hooked on the gear stick. I was a pretty lousy soldier! One of the gunmen then turned and took a shot at me, before the two of them were away on their bikes. I gave chase in the car, they split, so I followed the one that had fired at me, across the ford in the river and I knocked him off his bike. He dived into a dense orange grove and I managed to get out of the car and let off a few rounds in his direction, the first time that I had ever fired a sten gun! but he disappeared. I followed cautiously through the grove, not knowing what was on the other side. I came out of the grove to find the whole village lined up in front of me with no sign of the gunman. I had no option but to turn my back and return to my car, hoping that no one would put a bullet in my back. I arrived late at the office, reported what had happened and to my surprise I had a visit from the Military Police. They wanted to know if I had the empty cartridge cases to prove that I had fired them. I wanted to know if they were joking, but no, they insisted that I go back to where I had fired and find them, like a needle in a haystack! Well I did go back with four other squaddies, to put on a show, but the cases I produced came from another source?

It was following this incident that the Army decided Strovolo was not a safe village and I was eventually ordered to move. I was offered a quarter, but I had a shock when I went to see it and decided that no way would I live there. I did a proper Surveyor's report on the place and submitted it to the office with a memo to the effect that I would not live in it in UK, so certainly would not do so in Cyprus. Furthermore, my wife was pregnant, the external access stairs with 9-inch risers and no safety rail was not safe and I would send my wife home rather than impose that on her. This really put the cat among the pigeons and I was told that a Warrant Officer was the last occupant and I was only a Staff Sergeant. I refused to be browbeaten and said if I was forced to send my wife home the papers would certainly know the reason why. I was eventually offered an Officers Quarter at Palliourotisa Village, which I readily accepted, but I think my name was poison in the Mess.

Social life was becoming very restricted due to a ruling that all soldiers were required to be armed at all times. As my armament was a sten gun it meant that I had to be in uniform whenever I went out. A further restriction was imposed, which prevented other ranks from going through the manned barriers to leave Nicosia. This really annoyed me as we could no longer visit the night clubs on the Kyrenia Road and our only social life would be in the Sgts Mess? There was no restriction on Officers, who were armed with revolvers, so I then ordered a Beretta Pistol and 100 rounds, which I registered with the local police and used around 25 rounds getting used to the weapon. From then on we went wherever we wanted, in civvies but safely armed. Wearing my blazer and a cravat and driving the MG, I could drive up to any military barrier, flash any bit of paper, the barrier would go up and I would receive a salute as I drove through. I was never stopped to check that piece of paper.

With all the restrictions, guard duties etc. imposed to meet the terrorist threats, it was becoming very difficult to enjoy life. However we refused to be restricted and managed to continue sailing and enjoying whatever nightlife was available to be had. Barbara's pregnancy was to some extent a limitation, but she was very fit and we still managed to enjoy life. In fact her biggest problem seemed to be getting in and out of the MG, which she said was like trying to sit on the floor. She was crewing for me in the sailing dinghy only four days before giving birth to Vicki at the British Military Hospital Nicosia. I telephoned home to my family and Barbara's to tell them the news. To my surprise Laura said she already knew and told me at what time Vicki was born. Laura reckoned she had sympathetic pains at that time. I always said she was a bit of a lovable witch!

We were due to finish our tour of duty in Cyprus 16th December, but we were told that we would not be allowed to fly until Vicki was eight weeks old. I put the MG up for sale and it went in a week. I would have loved to have brought it home, but was persuaded that a draughty MG sports was hardly the transport for a new born baby in an English winter. We were happy to fly home early in the New Year, leaving, as we thought, all the problems behind. Approaching England, we were told that Stanstead airport was fogged in, so we had been diverted to an American Airbase in some out of the way place and we had another long delay waiting for coaches into London to be organised. With a very young baby, this was the last thing we wanted, but we did eventually get to London and on to Bristol. We went back to our room with Bert & Laura and enjoyed showing off our young daughter. I was then on leave till demob, for which I had to report to the RE camp near Salisbury. I bought an old Sunbeam Talbot drophead, which I daresay would have failed the current road test, but we needed transport. I reported to the camp 6th January 57, for demob on the 7th and was happy to say Goodbye to the Army way of life.

I soon realized that I had changed a lot during my time in the Army. I think I had grown up a lot and I came home with a much better understanding of myself and my capabilities. I had been working with Civilian Q S staff in Nicosia, I had asked lots of questions and had decided that a career in the Civil Service may well suit me. One very important factor was that we were never pressed to do overtime at short notice to meet a ridiculous dead line, as so often seemed to happen in private practice. My spare time was more important to me than the higher pay rates and furthermore I would be assured of a good pension. We had very much enjoyed our time in Cyprus before the trouble started and at that time there were many opportunities for employment in the many overseas stations in the dwindling British Empire. I had therefore applied to the Civil Service before leaving Cyprus and early in January 1957 I found myself appearing before a recruitment board in London. I had no idea what to expect, but first impression seemed quite formidable! There was a long table with Chairman and a secretary at the top and two other professional QSs each side. These four I found represented the Army, Air Force, Navy and Civil building departments. I was questioned pretty thoroughly on my experience in all aspects of QS work by all four professionals. Grade 3 post with Navy Works. I accepted the Grade 3 post with Navy Works at Milford Haven.

We agreed on the 26th February and I went down on my own initially by train, taking my bike with me and took a room in the town, whilst looking for accommodation. My landlady was a Tug Captains widow, her husband having drowned when his Tug hit a mine and she certainly fed me well. I had a huge fried breakfast every morning, which I could not fail to enjoy, except that she would always pour the fat from the pan onto the plate. Eventually I asked her if she would stop doing that and to my surprise she said "but that helps to keep the cold out". I told her that I had a cosy job in an office, not out on a tug. She was a real Dear and she did eventually get the message.

I was paid monthly, and with funds low I had to get some money in the bank before I could do very much. Borrowing money in those days was not the norm and I had been brought up with the idea that if you could not pay cash, you did without it. The Milford office was a small one comprising six QS staff and one clerical, d I found myself pretty busy, mainly at Brawdy. I had my bike, so I was soon getting in some training around the country lanes. I also wanted to find a weight training club, so I called at the local Police Station to enquire, as a lot of Police like to keep fit. I was told that the best man to talk to would be Yorri Evans, the Welsh Olympic Champion, who had represented Wales in the Empire Games and England in the Olympics, wow! I phoned Yorri, got a bit of a grilling about what I could lift and how keen was I. Then he invited me to join his small group in the boiler house of the school where he worked, for a trial session. I went along for the first training session and seemed to fit in alright, though I was the only office waller, the other four chaps were from farming, but I guessed I had passed the initial test. I remember one chap saying to me "I can see you are a gentleman by your shoes", you see, mine were polished, crazy! but it was nice. This was my introduction to Olympic type lifting, Press, Snatch and Clean & Jerk and before the end of the year I would be lifting in the Welsh Championship at Cardiff. I was very much a novice, but I was thrilled and it gave me new aspirations. Yorri was a very good influence and gave me some good advice on training, which enabled me to later become a local champion and a coach myself.

However, it would get us all together again and we could so the following weekend I heard that the Navy occasionally had spare quarters, unoccupied, I interested. We went to see it, Lounge, Kitchen and two bedrooms upstairs and only two miles from the office. We jumped at it I went home and brought Barbara & Vicki down in the battered old Sunbeam. and stayed there till we left Milford. It was an end house, right at the top of a hill and when the wind blew strong, as it often did, the metal windows rattled a tattoo, but we soon got used to that. Our next door neighbour we found was a fish buyer and he would often bring us in some unusual fish, which no one would buy because it was a rare type, but which he assured us was good eating. It was our first home where we really got settled, watching our first born growing up and we always remembered our Milford days with pleasure.

It was very much a fishing community in Milford and it was the regular thing for the trawler men to go to the pub on their return after a few days at sea. It was not uncommon to see wives berating their husbands, after dragging them out of the local before they could spend all their money. One day a fisherman was arrested for running around Milford in his underpants. Having arrived home in a bit of a drunken state, he had apparently stripped off and had a doze. He woke up and could not find his wife, so he went looking for her in the garden, she was not there, the door slammed and rather than wait he went looking for her down in the town!!

Most of my work was at Brawdy, an active Naval Air Station and I found myself walking miles when they resurfaced all the Runways and Taxiways and I measured the lot with one assistant and a Surveyor's chain. We had a lot of Irish labour on the site and they were pretty good workers. They also looked after one another and any one of them heading back to Ireland could be sure they would not go with empty pockets, as they would always have a whip around to see him off. As I arrived one day there was quite a commotion going on, as two of the Irish were having a punch up. The site Agent had each of them in his office to find out who started it, then told the culprit to collect his cards and be off the site by midday. A short while later the other one came to his office and said "I hear you have just sacked my best buddy, if he is going, I want my cards too". A rum but likeable lot! Another of my jobs there Involved the measurement of the new drainage system. I had had two labourers allocated to me, whose job it was to open up the manholes for me

Another activity of the weightlifting group was balancing and as I could walk on my hands, I fitted into that very well. Yorri was a brilliant balancer, he could do a one arm balance and was of course the top man of our five-man team. We put on several displays all over Pembrokeshire, always in aid of Charities. Initially we would do a demonstration of the three Olympic Lifts, Press, Snatch & Clean & Jerk, one chappie would break 6" nails with his bare hands, then we would do some half hour of team balancing. The finale would be our base man, lifting an anvil in his teeth while bending a steel bar around it, then swinging it from side to side. He would then get into reverse position on all fours with a 20ft plank on his chest. We would get some volunteers from the audience and get 10 men standing on the plank, very impressive. The show that really stands in my mind is the one at a small village near St David's. We had a wonderful welcome and a good audience. We got set upon the stage and did our usual one and half hour show with very good response. We were then surprised to be invited to stay for refreshment and even more surprised when they took the stage apart to provide the tables and we found that we had done our show on trestle tables. It was amazing that they had not collapsed and done someone an injury. On every occasion after that we always did an inspection of the stage before we started.

July 1978 Yorri was competing in the Empire Games in Cardiff and he invited Barbara & I to visit him at the village. He took us on a grand tour of the facilities and the following day we watched the mid heavy, light heavy and heavyweight competition. Yorri put up a good performance but missed out on medals, however the heavyweight division proved interesting. Ken McDonald, the British entry was the winner with a Clean & Jerk of 395lbs, the current British Record and he still had one lift left. Ken waved to say he was happy with that, but the crowd started shouting "We want 400". Three times he came out and shook his head, but the crowd kept up the chant. Eventually his coach came out and said OK Ken would have a go. When he came out for the lift you could have heard a pin drop as everyone was willing him to make it. He did a perfect lift to establish a new British Record and the theatre went wild. The current Mr Universe, Reg Parks rushed on stage, picked up Ken, all 14 stone and presented him to the crowd. What an ovation!

Work at the office was beginning to get a bit scarce. The Mine depot had been closed as it was now outdated, Brawdy Air Station was put into mothballs, being surplus to requirement after all the modernising that we had done to the place and Pembroke Dock was very old and little used. We were still doing estimates for various proposed works, but the powers that be did not seem inclined to spend any more money in our neck of the woods. I was getting very frustrated. I telephoned direct to the Chief QS, I told him about the work situation at Milford and that I was beginning to feel sorry that I had taken the post if there was no sign of a change. He thanked me and said that he would bear it in mind. Four weeks later he rang me to ask if I would be interested in a posting to Mauritius. I accepted straight away, then went home to find where Mauritius was. It looked like a tiny dot in the Indian Ocean, but sounded interesting.

Is it a dream?

Barbara was pregnant again and her doctor was not happy for her to travel as there appeared to be a few complications which needed watching, so I would have to travel out alone and Barbara would follow when she was considered fit. I was due to sail on the Stirling Castle from Southampton on 18th December. En-route to Cape Town.

 I found myself sharing a cabin with a recruit for the Rhodesian Police force. He was one of a group of ten and I was soon included in the group, so I was never without company. The following morning, we headed into Biscay, straight into a full Gale and our party was soon depleted.

 We arrived Cape Town on the 1st January 1959, and taken to the Alexandra Hotel. I was scheduled to sail on the M V Tegelburg on the 5th, so I hotfooted it down to the shipping office to collect my ticket. I was told that the ship had caught fire in Rio and was being repaired, so there would be a delay on the sailing date and would I please come back next week. I was not carrying enough cash to pay the hotel for another week Visa and Bank cards had not been thought of in those days and transfer of cash had to be arranged through banks and took a while. He understood the problem and advanced me sufficient cash to pay my bills, so I rested easier that night. There were a couple of fellows I had known on the ship who were staying in Cape Town for a few days before moving on north, so we teamed up, hired a car and did some exploring around the Cape. We stopped at the Dolls House for tea, where pretty girls on roller skates provide you with trays to attach to the car door and bring your food to the car. That evening we drove to a Drive-in Cinema, where you park your car in lots in front of a massive screen and bring a speaker into the car. It was a novel experience, but a bit chaotic when everyone was trying to leave at the same time. It was a fantastic Gym with separate White and Black areas, the apartheid being very apparent at that time. I talked to Whites, Afrikaners and Blacks and it was clear that there was a lot mistrust and lack of understanding between them. I came away feeling happy that I had decided against emigration.

I boarded the Tegelberg on 13th January 1959 and met Stan Ruecroft and his family, Stan was a dour Yorkshire man and would be my boss for the next three years, but we got on well. There were very few English aboard and the few that were seemed to spend most of their time playing bridge. However, there were a lot of young, active French people on board, so I sat on the deck with my French book, revising all the french that I had not used since leaving Grammar School. I was sitting on deck in the sun, muttering french when I heard a voice say "Ah monsieur, vous practice le francais". I replied "Qui, je parle un peu". Her name was Roselys Thevenau returning from a holiday in South Africa and within a few hours I had been introduced to her brother, Jeane Claude and friends, Jozianne & Ada all from Mauritius, It did a great deal toward making my trip a very pleasant one and as it turned out, the start of some wonderful friendships.(Mum and dad met up with them again in 2003)

We stopped at Port Elizabeth where I went ashore with Bert, an Afrikaner, to visit a friend of his, but I found the town very dull and uninviting. The next stop was in Durban, where we stopped for two days. I enjoyed my visit, taking a coach trip to the Valley of a thousand hills and a Zulu Reservation, followed by Ngoma Native dancing, a very colourful and vigorous display that made the ground shake. The last night aboard we sailed past Reunion Island and the partying went on till 01.30, with a passenger on the piano and plenty of sing along. It was a wonderful end to six glorious weeks, which can only be described as a paid holiday and I was truly looking forward to getting stuck into some work.

We anchored in Port Louis, Mauritius on Sunday, 25th January, 1959, where I was met by another quantity surveyor. He rushed me off the ship, assuming that my baggage would follow me and took me to his home for breakfast, then on to the Park Hotel at Curepipe, which would be my home for a while. He waited while I changed to more casual clothes, then whisked me off again to meet his family and then on to Blue Bay for a wonderful day on the beach, what a life! The very next day I was at the office to start work after six glorious weeks of pleasure and meet the rest of my working colleagues. I was told that the contract which I would be responsible for would not be starting for a further three weeks, as I had arrived earlier than expected. However, in the meantime I could be usefully employed helping out on another contract. I enquired about the rest of my luggage and was rather put out to hear that my large travelling trunk and the box containing my weights were still on the ship, on its way to Singapore. It was several weeks before I saw them again and in the meantime I had only that which was in my hand luggage, so it was necessary to do a bit of shopping.

His story ends there but his life carried on until 10 September 2019 aged 89 with many adventures in the meantime

THE END

BIBLIOGRAPHY and references

Most of the material in this book is available online but trying to gather it all together in times of stress can be difficult. I hope this book makes it easier for you to access the right material to help you on your way

I used the following sites

https://www.alzheimers.org.uk/about-us/news-and-media/facts-media

https://www.dementiauk.org/

www.telecarechoice.co.uk/

https://www.ageuk.org.uk

www.cqc.org.uk

www.which.co.uk

https://www.nhs.uk/conditions/end-of-life-care/advance-statement/

https://www.seniorlink.com

Health - BBC News - https://www.bbc.com › news › health

Daily mail

https://dementia.livebetterwith.com

Which?   - https://magazine.which.co.uk

Photo – originator Vernon Wills

Thank you to Julia and Mary (Nurses in dads care home) you know who you are, who gave me the confidence to try to publish. Thanks to Hazel for proof reading. Thank you to my other half Simon and my Sons for helping and putting up with my silence, highs and lows throughout the adventure.